THE
Faces
OF
Gifted

A resource for educators and parents

By Nancy L. Johnson

Pieces of Learning

Division of Creative Learning Consultants

© 1989 **Pieces of Learning**
Division of Creative Learning Consultants Inc.

Cover: Jim Rohal Design

ISBN No. 0-9623835-0-3
Printing No. 98765

Table of Contents

PREFACE

The first face was Brian's. He whirled into my classroom and into my life one rainy November day in 1968. To say that my life hasn't been the same is truly an understatement. Like most gifted children, Brian was a puzzle — many pieces, each unique. He was both a source of great joy and intense frustration. A fascinating dichotomy of nonstop energy. This was a child who could describe in great detail what his Aunt Bertha wore at Christmas three years before, but couldn't tell me where he laid his pencil two minutes before!! Because of Brian, my interest in gifted children grew rapidly. There have been many faces since Brian's and many new puzzle pieces. *THE Faces OF Gifted* is a collection of articles that originally appeared in CHALLENGE magazine. Each article is offered as a piece to the "gifted puzzle," to be touched, turned, examined, and otherwise re-defined. Put together, the pieces form a beginning picture of the many faces of gifted children. Perhaps readers will find a special piece, once missing, that will lead to a better understanding of his or her own experience with gifted children.

NLJ

PERFECT

I am someone tried and true,
I'm sure you'd like to know me.
They tell me I'm a gifted child,
Grown-ups want to own me.
I'm honest as the day is long,
Just as sweet as pie.
Good as gold, right as rain,
The apple of your eye.
I'm just as quick as lightning,
Busy as a bee I am,
Pretty as a picture,
And as happy as a clam.
I'm quiet as a door mouse.
Sharp as any tack,
Bright as a new penny,
Wise as an owl in fact.

And then the other side of me,
As stubborn as a mule,
Mean as any junkyard dog,
Breaking every rule.
Angry as an old, wet hen,
Sly as any fox,
Crazy as a bedbug,
A face for stopping clocks!
As slippery as an eel,
Sneaky as a snake,
Mad as any hornet,
Nutty as a fruitcake.
Now you know both sides,
The sour and the sweet,
Which one of the two of me,
Would you like to meet?

from *Don't Burn Down the Birthday Cake*

by Joe Wayman

I dedicate this book

to my father, John G. Johnson whose love, strength, and support continue each day

and

to the loving memory of my mother, V. Frances Johnson whose love for children is reflected in my life and in the pages of this book.

A special thanks to Joe Wayman, musician, author, poet, first editor of CHALLENGE, and friend extraordinaire

and

Kathy and Stan Balsamo for all the "spit and polish" on the manuscript

and

Brian, who wouldn't let me make him average.

Introduction

Gifted Perspectives

An Interview with Nancy L. Johnson by Kathy Balsamo

Parent meetings attracted 10-15 parents years ago. Nancy now finds it is not unusual for 200 parents to attend a meeting. Parents are becoming very knowledgeable. They attend workshops, are educated, read, and are coming to schools with "ammunition," expecting better things for their children.

Nancy sees changes in parenting roles, relationships, and attitudes toward children, educators, and the gifted curriculum.

A CULTURAL MIRROR

"We try to use the schools to change our society, and I believe it's the opposite. It has always been a reflection. Our schools reflect our economy, our society, and our culture. Look into any classroom in this country, and you are looking at culture and all the advantages and problems that go with it. If it's neat to be gifted in Podunk-in that town-it will be neat to be gifted in that school.

Implications of Today's Family Structure

First, in two parent families both parents usually work. The traditional family unit with Mom being home is disappearing. That fact affects education in general and therefore affects gifted education.

We're beginning to understand that some women **can** do it all; some can have a family and a career. Others cannot. It's not a weakness. These women have found that they have to quit their jobs; or they have to have a career, stop it for awhile and be a mother and a wife, and then return to their careers.

Secondly, in the past, children had a role model of one parent being the achiever, mainly Dad. Even though Mom was achieving, it didn't appear the same. The child who has a role model of **two** people achieving receives a double whammy. Many high-achieving parents do not realize the stress for gifted children. We're seeing students who say to us, 'There's no way I can be as good as my parents. I can't do more.'

5

Students can react to change and the pressure to achieve in very powerful ways. I see a tension, a constant tension, that some gifted children **are** able to handle. Frequently we are recommending that gifted children take Karate lessons and do physical things—jogging—to get the body going because that will relieve the tension. They're like a rubber band, constantly being stretched tight. That's a reaction to the constant tension to achieve. Some **don't** handle tension well. They end up anorexic and have serious emotional problems, eating problems, or run away, attempt, and commit suicide.

Most of us were raised in the 50s by parents who wanted more for their children. We grew up in an economy that was constantly building. People made more money and bought a house. When you sold it, you sold it for more money. Everything was constantly building. Salaries were constantly going up. However, that leveled off. No longer are salaries building, and the minimum wage hasn't been raised since the 1950s!

But parents' hopes for their children are the same today.

We now have young people with families who, because they cannot 'make it,' are moving back with Mom and Dad who have a house that is paid for.

A fourth change involves *Supermoms* and *Superdads* who are both working and clawing their way to the top of the corporate ladder. Psychologists tell us we should be supportive of children, be there to guide them and help them, but don't dictate the outcome of their lives. It's hard for these high achieving parents, these *Supermoms* and *Superdads,* not to do that, especially when they know the child has potential.

So, not only do they want to be supportive, but they want to say, 'This child is going to the Harvard Medical School.'

Another significant change is the number of older parents who have younger children. Women who were not going to have children at 30 decided at 35 to have children. Those students are in K-4th and 5th grades. Many of the families are two parents with jobs and only one or two children. All the eggs are in one basket. They get THE attention, THE focus. Most of these parents are more emotionally and financially secure having their first child at 30. Thus, these children get a different kind of start than with a parent 21 years old with no money.

And lastly, we have young unmarried parents, welfare mothers, and single parents. There's a bit of a desperation sometimes. The single parent over tries, overdoes. There's a feeling of 'I'm it'. One parent is trying to compensate for two parents. That is accentuated when the child is gifted.

Shifting Interaction and the Extended Family

We're seeing baby boomer parents who don't just put their children into ANY daycare or ANY pre school. They look for a **gifted** pre school. They look for day cares that will prepare these children and will give them two or three rungs up on the ladder when they get into school.

I believe we're now into a different kind of extended family. It used to be Mother was the main nurturer. She was there and spent the most time with the children. Now we have fathers taking over more nurturing.

Daycare and pre school people—the new extended family—are interacting with the child more in a day's time than Mother.

Another interaction for some children is TV. So the interaction has changed to involve other kinds of interaction, not just Mom.

Mobility

In addition to the stress of having two parents as high achievers, many gifted children have the stress of moving a lot. Although mobility was forced on some, many more are choosing it.

Now there are people who deliberately move to places like Fairfax County, Virginia, because of the schools. Parents are asking to be moved to schools with specific gifted programs.

Martha Collins, former Kentucky governor, stated Kentucky had to improve education in the state so the state could pull in more industry. She did it. And she was right. Kentucky has better schools and more industry. People are deliberately moving into some areas.

And because we are a mobile society, because we HAVE to be, and because we WANT to be, there are all kinds of fringe stresses that add to the stress of high achievement.

PARENTS AND THE SCHOOLS

Parents previously held teachers and administrators on a pedestal. With that pedestal came intimidation. Parents accepted what the school, program, and teacher said.

Now we have parents who are more educated and are asking more questions.

For economic reasons, we've had to pass bond issues. Intimidating had to stop. Telling parents has stopped and asking them has started. Parents are like consumers of education. Administrators now have parents coming in and interviewing them wanting to know, 'Do you have this kind of program?' Because parents are shopping around for schools, administrators are having to deal with parents as consumers.

We have parents who are coaches for Odyssey of the Mind, who go to training sessions for Jr. Great books, and who are more directly involved in the educational process.

I see an effort to focus on both home and school. **We are all in this together.** Administrators realize that's where the power is. They are coming to grips with the fact that parents are not adversaries, that educators are not sitting on pedestals, and that educators can't tell parents 'this is what your child needs; do what we say.' **We're in gifted education together.**

Parents have found out what parents of other special education children have known for years. Those parents said, 'Wait a minute!' and suddenly there were laws. Now, parents of gifted children are saying, 'Hey wait a minute!'

WHAT GIFT HAS GIFTED GIVEN US?

We have some solid gifted/talented programs that have existed for 15-20 years. We're beginning to see that not only does the gifted program benefit this small group of gifted children, but there is a *spill over* effect.

When you teach teachers what to do with gifted children, you're teaching them how to be better teachers. You don't teach them to do the same things for ALL students. But you teach teachers to be more confident, to keep growing, to keep learning, keep taking classes. Gifted Education keeps teachers motivated.

That motivation spills over into all children, and there is a *spill over* effect in curriculum. When you improve the curriculum for gifted children, you begin to focus on the whole curriculum. If we need to be doing more creative thinking skills for gifted children, do we need to be doing more creative thinking skills for all children?

THE FUTURE

Minority gifted—we have to do a better job of identifying and providing programs for them.

We have to get business and industry more involved in education. Public school systems are not able to pay educators enough to keep them out of industry. We have a lot of small school districts which cannot afford to hire the variety of people we need to meet the needs of gifted children. We don't have the trained personnel in education to meet some of the high-level needs of gifted students who are gifted in certain areas. We need to use local industry for mentoring.

There is a trend. We are expanding pull-out programs to cover the social and emotional needs of gifted children; clustering gifted children in a support system; schools for gifted children who don't fit into our gifted programs.

Changing Curriculum: Nose to Nose

Tannenbaum speaks of the difference between programs for the gifted: **comprehensive**—sequential parts of the school's curriculum, and **provisions** for the gifted—short, fragmented supplements to the school's curriculum.

I worry about gifted students who are sitting nose to screen instead of nose to nose, learning to work together, learning from another human, learning to work with, and getting along with, someone who works in a different learning style.

Needed: Life Support Skills

In recent years we have learned that offering gifted students high-level academics is good, but it's not enough. In the future we will be focusing on using academics to teach how to deal with frustration.

We are finding more and more gifted students insulating themselves from challenge and frustration. They are literally sliding through their academics without ever being challenged or frustrated. They reach adulthood, get their first C in college, lose their first job, and don't know what to do. These are the 'kids' who run away and can't handle it. Perhaps somewhere in their childhood we didn't stimulate them on a high enough level.

I don't want them to be afraid. Some of the best thinking they will ever do as a human will come out of challenge and frustration. Understand it, but don't be afraid of it.

I've worked with the best and the brightest in a school situation, and some students can't think their way out of a paper bag because there aren't any written instructions in a textbook. 'What are you going to do when you get out into life and there isn't a textbook that tells you what to do? And you aren't going to get a grade? What if you have to do it just because you want to?' I ask them. Break mind sets. Train your brain to look at things in a different way.

Social/Emotional Needs of Gifted: Safe and Unsafe Rebellion

We have to support, offer, suggest, and accept some safe rebellion from children.

Many gifted children begin rebelling about 4th grade. They may turn to unsafe rebellion—experimenting with drugs and alcohol and sex. Perhaps tolerating an amount of smart mouth, green fuzzy things that grow under the bed because the room hasn't been cleaned for a month, and a pierced ear is necessary because of the alternatives.

Parents of fifteen years ago, who would never accept purple hair, now may need to. When my generation was growing up, if someone ran away from home, he got so far and somebody would give him a ride home. Or he would get hungry and ask to be taken home. Now when a child runs away, he gets on a bus, on a plane, or if someone picks him up, it may be tragic. He may find himself in places that are mind boggling.

Children rebel because they don't have power. They don't have rights. We need to give children ways to **express** power. When you have power as a human being you're worth something. How do they have it in the classroom and at home? **Modeling**...practice what you preach...model the power of high-level thinking...consistently...over a long period...if you want your children to be a life-long learner, you be a life-long learner.

Looking Ahead

Research from Ohio says we must prepare children for at least ten job changes and three careers in a lifetime. Most will change five times. Every eight years a typical gifted adult wants and needs to change careers. How do you deal with this restlessness every eight years, and what if you don't want to be a lawyer any more and want to go to California and be a cowboy? How are you going to deal with that? Solutions include dealing with challenge, frustration, breaking mind sets, switching gears, and learning to work with other people. It begins at the elementary level.

A PARTING COMMENT

I'm optimistic. I believe that parents and educators are learning that gifted is more than just academics; that we have to look at the whole child; that developing the child's intellectual abilities on the gifted level isn't going to do the child any good if he/she emotionally and physically can't survive. Gifted and Talented *Programs* are the job of a few people.

Gifted and Talented Education is Everyone's job.

A GARDEN OF GIFTS

a privileged view because folks had to make a special trip, sometimes driving several miles, just to enjoy for a few moments what my family experienced every time we looked out the window. Yes, Charlie's garden was a famous place, at least it seemed that way, to a child growing up in a small town. However, I never really appreciated the significance of Charlie and his flower garden until years later when I became a teacher working with gifted children.

You see, a visit to Charlie's garden involved more than just looking at the flowers. It involved Charlie. He took great pride in his garden and enjoyed talking about it to whomever would listen. The flowers were his only family, each variety like a special child with its own distinct beauty and unique growing needs, size, shape, and color. Because Charlie lived a good many years, had experienced a lot, and had learned a lot, every comment came with bits of wisdom, advice, and lessons about life and people. And whether Charlie knew it or not, he was a marvelous teacher. He answered all of a little girl's persistent and never-ending questions with loving patience.

"What kind of flower is this, Charlie? Tell me about this one! Tell me about that one!" He would begin with a basic description of each particular flower: the name, variety, growing cycle, etc. But he always concluded the "lesson" with the same statement: "Ya know, Missy, flowers are a lot like people, and this one reminds me of. . ." Of course, no one ever left Charlie's garden without a bouquet, a handful of memories.

For almost ten of my childhood years, visits to Charlie's garden marked changes of the four seasons. The kitchen window in our house provided a perfect view of Charlie's house and his adjoining flower garden. It was

Well, Charlie is gone now, and a new house sits on the ground where his garden once grew. Somehow that seems OK. The garden and Charlie may be gone, but the images of those beautiful flowers, that patient teacher, and the important lessons about life and people remain.

Just like Charlie's flowers, gifted children come in all sizes, shapes, and colors. In an effort to better understand the characteristics of gifted children, let's visit Charlie's garden.

MARIGOLDS

Marigolds are tough, no-nonsense flowers. They don't have a sweet, pleasant smell—a characteristic that makes them unique among flowers. As Charlie would say, "Marigolds are for lookin,' not for smellin'!" To say they are tough is an understatement. From too much rain to total drought, the marigold will survive. For the beginning gardener, they are a sure thing. Marigolds don't need lots of fussing over and attention, just an occasional weeding. They seem to grow in spite of us!

Marvin is a tough, no-nonsense, gifted child. It may be said that he is easy to love but hard to like. He constantly challenges the ideas and values of adults, and he asks "hard" questions. "Why do people get into wars?" "When the snow melts, where does the white go?"

"Why do kids have to go to school until they are sixteen?" "Why are there so many starving people and fat people in the world?" "Why can't kids vote?" WHY! WHY! WHY!

Although Marvin is constantly questioning his world, he is a confident, self-reliant child because his parents have built an emotional support system around him. They don't al-ways have the magic answers to his questions, but they do have a sympathetic attitude toward his curiosity. Marvin is a persistent, goal-directed, sometimes stubborn, gifted child who is determined to learn and find out things in spite of us. And just like the marigold, Marvin will survive.

DAISIES

The daisy, a member of the chrysanthemum family, is an old-fashioned flower that is a favorite of many people. Its delicate white petals have been the inspiration for many a poet and songwriter. It's a gentle flower with a long, pliable stem. Over the years, the daisy has been the symbol for all flowers. If you ask a person to draw a flower, results are usually a close facsimile to the daisy.

Daisies seem to do best when they are growing with other daisies. They seem to gain strength from each other. In Charlie's words, "One daisy is pretty, but a whole bunch is beautiful!" Daisies are particularly appropriate for cutting and make lovely bouquets.

Debbie is a sensitive, intuitive, gifted child. Her creativeness and energy are a constant source of amazement to her parents. Since the age of three, she has demonstrated unusual abilities in the visual and performing arts. She draws, paints, sings, and dances! Quite often she combines all of her talents by writing, directing, and acting her own ten-minute drama productions. Her teacher has commented several times on the originality of her oral expression. Her responses are unusual, clever, and unique: "Maybe if we put detergent in the birdbath, all the birds will come and take a bubble bath!"

Debbie's parents have supported her growing talents by enrolling her in private music lessons as well as gymnastics. Just as daisies seem to do best when they are growing with other daisies, Debbie enjoys learning in groups with other children who have similar talents. Among the many activities that Debbie enjoys, cooking is one of her favorites. It was no surprise to her parents when she announced that she had decided what she was going to be when she grows up. "I'm going to be a chef who dances, directs, sings, and writes novels!" Yes, just as many people relate the image of all flowers to that daisy, Debbie fits the image that many people have of gifted children.

SUNFLOWERS

According to Charlie, sunflowers are the biggest, tallest, heaviest, and fastest-growing flowers in the garden. But more than anything else, they are proud flowers. "I always feel like standing at attention when I look at those giants!" said Charlie.

Sunflowers need thick, strong stems to support their heavy, round tops. The tops are full of seeds which make them a real attraction to birds. Sunflowers are truly "sun flowers." They literally follow the sun, bending and turning those heavy tops, continually searching for their place in the sun.

Sasha is a leader. She looks like one, talks like one, and acts like one. Sasha accepts responsibility with ease. She gets good grades in school and is a member of most clubs and honors organizations. She is often chosen by other children to be the leader, and she attracts followers like the sunflower attracts birds. Sometimes she carries her role as leader little too far and dominates others. She has an uncanny ability to sense right and wrong. And to her father's embarrassment, she occasionally corrects adults when she thinks they are wrong! Like most parents of "born leaders," Sasha's father worries about her occasional bossy behavior. He realizes that his daughter needs guidance and direction, and just as the sunflower must follow the sun, Sasha must also learn that there are times to follow as well as lead.

Sasha is very sensitive to the feelings of others and worries about the responsibility of being a leader. Right now, her goal in life is to go into politics. Will Sasha find her place in the sun?

QUEEN ANNE'S LACE

Queen Anne's Lace is a wild plant of the carrot family, with fine leaves and small, delicate white flowers in flat-topped clusters. Most people would never consider it a real flower. To most it is just a weed, something you cut down or spray to get rid of—a plant of little value.

But sure enough, there it is, growing in Charlie's garden. A surprise! A surprise, that is, to everyone but Charlie. You see, Charlie saw things in Queen Anne's Lace that nobody else could see. The sparkle in his eyes as he gently touched the blossoms told everyone that this was his favorite flower. Few people realized that hiding behind the label "weed" was a beautiful and important flower. Queen Anne's Lace has large carrot-like roots that not only hold moisture but also hold the soil and keep it from eroding. It also has a strong smell that serves as a natural insect repellent. And it can be enjoyed year-round because the blossoms can be dried and used for bouquets in the winter. As Charlie would say,"The good Lord probably put 'the Lace' here on earth just to test us to see if we could uncover all those surprises!"

Larry is a child filled with hidden surprises. Just as it is difficult for some people to consider Queen Anne's Lace a flower, it is difficult to consider Larry a gifted child. In fact, he has been labeled everything but gifted: underachiever, learning disabled, and behavior problem.

The surprises hidden inside Larry come to the surface in the form of contradictions. He is achieving three grade levels above in math and science but is barely average in English. He has a smart brain, and a smart mouth! He spends hours in his bedroom working with a chemistry set, but never seems interested in doing homework. He seems to have an unusually long attention span and excellent powers of concentration, but hates routine, drill, and test taking to prove what he knows. He enjoys talking to adults about scientific things but is very skeptical of those who try to give him advice and tell him what to do. He hates English but has written some beautiful poetry.

Behind all these contradictions is a bright, sensitive gifted child. IF he is lucky, Larry will be discovered by a teacher who sees his potential, accepts him as a gifted child, and then provides for his special needs. IF he is lucky, Larry will have parents who believe in him and who will work hard to help establish a gifted program in their son's school. IF he is lucky, Larry will find another gifted person (a mentor) to help him better understand what it means to be gifted-what it means to be a weed trying to blossom in the middle of the flower garden.

There are so many flowers left in the garden. We have just begun to understand, enjoy, and appreciate their significance.

As long as there are gardens,

As long as there are Charlies,

and as long as there are curious little girls,

there is hope—hope for our most precious resource—GIFTED CHILDREN!

WHO IS GIFTED?

Identification of Gifted Children

Like many beginning teachers, the term "gifted child" meant very little to me. There were few undergraduate education courses that dealt with special learners and none that dealt with gifted education. I did complete one general special education class. As I remember, the last chapter in the book dealt with the needs of gifted children, but we never managed to get to it. I vaguely remember the instructor saying, "Don't worry about your gifted kids; they will make it anyway. You will have enough trouble with your slow learners."

So the term 'gifted education' got tucked away in the back of my head along with other bits of educational jargon. I finished college and entered the field of teaching feeling well-qualified and prepared to join my fellow educators.

Then one cold October day, along came Brian, and my whole life was turned upside down!

WHO IS GIFTED?

It's not an easy question to answer. The experts don't agree. Some definitions seem too narrow and leave out many truly gifted children; others are too broad, and before you know it, every child fits the criteria. If one digs deep and long enough, one can find research to support almost any position. It is important to remember that the definition of *gifted* fits your community and your school. The following definitions have been used in the past to identify gifted children:

1. gifted (gif' tid) adj: having a natural ability or aptitude; talented; notably superior in intelligence.

2. A gifted and/or talented person demonstrates or has the potential for excellence in some field of constructive human endeavor. Such fields include, but are not limited to, academics, aesthetics, kinesthetics, athletics, and human relations.

14

3. The U.S. Office of Education, when in existence, under the direction of Public Law 91-230, Section 806, established the following definition for purposes of federal education programs. Many districts still use this definition today.

- Gifted and talented children are those identified by professional qualified persons who, by virtue of outstanding abilities, are capable of high performance. These are children who require differentiated educational programs and/or services beyond those normally provided by the regular school program in order to realize their contribution to self and society. Children capable of high performance include those with demonstrated achievement and/or potential ability in any of the following areas, singly or in combination:

General Intellectual Ability

Specific Academic Aptitude

Creative or Productive Thinking

Leadership Ability

Visual and Performing Arts

A clearer understanding of the federal definition can be found in examining each talent area:

- **General Intellectual Ability:** The child possessing general intellectual ability is consistently superior to that of other children in the school to the extent that there is a need and the child can profit from specially planned educational services beyond those normally provided by the standard school program.

- **Specific Academic Aptitude:** The child possessing a specific academic aptitude is that child who has an aptitude in a specific subject area that is consistently superior to the aptitudes of other children in the school to the extent that there is a need and the child can profit from specially planned educational services beyond those normally provided by the standard school program.

- **Creative/Productive Thinking:** The creative thinking child is that child who consistently engages in divergent thinking that results in unconventional responses to conventional tasks to the extent that there is a need and the child can profit from specially planned educational services beyond those normally provided by the standard school program.

- **Leadership Ability:** The child possessing leadership ability is that child who not only assumes leadership roles, but also is accepted by others as a leader to the extent that there is a need and the child can profit from specially planned educational services beyond those normally provided by the standard school program.

- **Visual and Performing Arts Ability:** The child possessing visual and performing arts ability is that child who consistently produces outstanding aesthetic productions in graphic arts, sculpture, music, or dance and needs and can profit from specially planned educational services beyond those normally provided by the standard school program.

4. Gifted and Talented: Those children and young people whose abilities, talents, and potential for accomplishment are so outstanding that they require special provisions to meet their educational needs.

15

5. A gifted child is one who, due to superior intellect (IQ of 130 or higher), advanced learning ability (testing in the top 95% or 9th stanine on achievement tests), or both, is not given the opportunity to progress and develop in the regular classroom and needs special instruction and services.

6. Gifted and Talented Children: Those children who excel in their ability to think, solve problems, evaluate data, create, and invent new ideas. Children with these abilities require special educational provisions; i.e., facilities and/or services provided by the local educational agency.

- **Question:** Do the definitions describe a gifted child as a "good worker"?

Remember: Not all gifted children are "good workers" or "good grade-getters"; 10% of those children who drop out of school are highly gifted.

- **Question:** Do the definitions describe gifted children as attractive, well-behaved, conforming children?

Remember: A gifted child does not have perfect behavior. Sometimes gifted children are discipline problems.

- **Question:** Is the phrase "has a high IQ" used in the definition?

Remember: An individual IQ test has a margin of error of 10 to 15 points.

- **Question:** Do the definitions reflect a positive or negative attitude toward gifted children?

Remember: Americans are notorious in their attitude toward the "underdogs" of society. Gifted children are not thought of as underdogs. Many people believe that gifted children will make it in our society without special help. The fact is that gifted children

DON'T make it anyway. **They learn to be average.**

CHARACTERISTICS OF GIFTED

Now try formulating your own definition of gifted.

The following characteristics of gifted children might help you in the identification process:

A gifted child:

- Questions critically.
- Memorizes easily.
- Transfers learning to new situations.
- Learns rapidly and easily.
- Does some academic work two years in advance.
- Uses a large number of words easily and accurately.
- Visualizes mentally.
- Shows curiosity and originality.
- Has a wide range of interests.
- Is an avid reader.
- Has the power of abstraction, conceptualization, and synthesis.
- Solves problems and processes ideas in a complex way.
- Has a sense of humor.
- May have a long attention span.
- Seems to have more emotional stability.
- Sometimes comes up with unexpected, even "silly" answers.
- Is often asked by peers for ideas and suggestions.
- Is a good listener.
- Understands and accepts reasons for change.

- Anticipates outcomes.
- Is challenged by new ideas.
- Likes to improvise.
- Offers several solutions to the same problem.
- Shows ability to plan, organize, execute, and judge.
- Uses trial-and-error methods.
- Finds ways to extend ideas.
- Seems to know when, where, and how to seek help.
- Makes generalizations.
- Is perceptually open to the environment.
- Is sensitive to the feelings of others or to situations.
- May sometimes dominate peers or situations.
- Is persistent.
- Has a high energy level.
- May have an imaginary playmate.
- Gets excited about learning new ideas.
- Exercises responsibilities independently.
- Perceives and articulates the unstated feelings of others.

Can you add any characteristics to this list?

Brian didn't possess all of the listed characteristics, but his profile did include many interesting possibilities. Some statements indicated Brian was gifted, while others simply described a typical first grader. Like all gifted children, Brian had two sets of peers—intellectual peers and age peers. He possessed some of the characteristics of both.

For example, Brian:
- Asked questions constantly.
- Seemed to understand books, films, and discussions at a much "deeper" level.
- Tried to be a perfectionist—hated to fail.
- Worried about adult issues and problems.
- Possessed super concentration—seemed to "get lost" in books and activities.
- Loved the library/learning center (had a crush on the librarian!)
- Gave his opinion about things whether asked or not.
- Always had a better way of doing things.

- Liked to make people laugh—a dry sense of humor.
- Had poor handwriting.
- Loved to read, read, read!
- Seemed very sensitive to his environment.

- Was not always sociable—liked to work independently.

- Performed at least two years above grade level in most content areas.

- Scored 149 on an IQ test.

- Had extremes in moods.

- Wanted to take part in activities with his age peers.

- Was always "two jumps" ahead of his teacher.

- Accepted responsibility from adults.

- Was always full of energy.

Now think about your gifted child. List some of the characteristics that seem to fit your child.

IDEAS TO CONSIDER IN THE IDENTIFICATION PROCESS

Gifted children come from ALL socio-economic and cultural levels. The identification process should include special provisions for cultural minorities. Because of differences in cultural backgrounds and experiences, minority children may not score high enough on a standardized test to qualify for the gifted program. As a result, many highly gifted minority children are missed during the identification process. Sometimes standardized test scores are weighted to ensure more minority gifted children are identified.

As the identification process progresses, consider the following:

1. At home, look for different types of strengths in your child. Observe the different areas of giftedness.

2. Does the school inform you about the identification process and the special programs available?

3. In your school, is your child first identified and then a program planned? Or, are students identified for a program already in existence?

4. Does the school use information already available that would be helpful in identifying your child—cumulative records, achievement tests, parent inventory, IQ scores?

5. Is there a preliminary screening of students to form a pool from which final selection is made? Are there pre-established definitions and criteria? Is 5 to 10 percent of the school population considered for a gifted program?

6. Is a summary sheet used to make the final selection? Does it include a compilation of scores from identification instruments? Are particularly important scores assigned a weight?

7. Is your child labeled "gifted" or "potentially gifted"? What is the difference?

SOME FINAL THOUGHTS ON IDENTIFICATION

1. It is important that all students be included in the identification process. Many potentially gifted students are missed because they were not included in the initial screening process.

2. The entire identification process must be repeated every year. A child who is growing up gifted is constantly stretching and changing in different directions. A gifted child who is missed one year might be discovered the next year if identification is repeated.

3. All people who have information about the child being considered for the gifted program should be involved in the identification procedure (parents, student, speech teacher,

guidance counselor, librarian, classroom teachers, and administrators).

4. Students need to be identified with a variety of instruments. The tools of identification might include standardized tests, reports, interviews from professional people, conferences with the student, achievement test scores, past grades, personal history

questionnaires, home visits with parents, extra curricular activities, student interest inventories, creativity tests, parent inventories, anecdotal records, situational tasks, daily logs or journals of things done by the student, cumulative records, affective tests, sociometric data, or teacher checklists.

Those instruments used most often are group and individual intelligence tests, teacher recommendation using a checklist, parent inventory, past school records, achievement tests, and peer identification.

5. Although most gifted programs use specific cutoff points on standardized tests or percentages of the population as part of the identification process, it is important that students not be ruled out because of one low test score. The identification procedure should be flexible enough to incorporate the use of

multiple criteria and instruments so students can qualify for the program in a number of ways.

6. There are gifted children waiting to be identified in each grade level. However, middle grade children are easier to identify and fewer mistakes are made in the process.

7. The identification process is not complete until all those educators involved have discussed the results with those students identified as gifted. Many educators shy away from this task because they fear the use of the word "gifted." Whether you call them the smart kids, the high class, the bluebirds, or the buzzards, the fact is that a gifted child is a gifted child. Sometime, somehow, someone must sit down with that child and talk about what it means to be gifted. Trying to hide the word 'gifted' from the child only increases the problems. So, talk about it! Talk with the gifted child and talk with his or her peers. How does it feel to be gifted? What does it mean to have a friend who is gifted? Being gifted doesn't mean you are better than anyone else; it means you are DIFFERENT. Gifted kids are kids first and gifted second.

GIFTED PRESCHOOLERS

Children of Promise

In a 1983 survey of 1,000 parents of gifted children, Nancy Eberle found 87 percent "first suspected" that their children were gifted before the children entered kindergarten. Twenty-two percent guessed during their children's first 12 months of life; 48 percent, between the ages of one and three; 17 percent, between four and five years; and 13 percent, when their children were older. Parents continue to be excellent identifiers of gifted preschool children. They recognize many of the characteristics of giftedness that begin to "pile up" at an early age.

A GIFTED PRESCHOOLER:

- Has an unusual memory.
- Walks and talks early.
- Teaches himself/herself to read.
- Offers several solutions to the same problem.
- Recites from memory.
- Has a large vocabulary.
- Solves problems and processes ideas in a complex way (high-level thinking).
- Has an almost adult sense of humor.
- Has a long attention span.
- Exercises responsibilities .
- Perceives and articulates the unstated feelings of others.
- Is persistent.
- Shows curiosity and originality.
- Worries about adult issues and problems.
- Has a high energy level.
- Gives his/her opinions about things, whether asked or not.
- Is not always sociable—likes to do things independently and to be alone.
- Asks questions constantly.
- Seems to understand books, films, and discussions at a much "deeper" level.
- Is a nonstop talker!

Expect the characteristics to surface in clusters. Unfortunately, when they do, the resulting behaviors from the gifted preschooler are not always socially acceptable. A case in point: Meet Tony.

Tony*

by Kaye Starbird

Tony's drying dishes and cleaning out the hall,
And all he did was use the phone to make a friendly call.

For Tony's being punished (which happens more and more)
Because he's only four years old and much too smart for four.
A case of what I mean is this; his parents thought it prattle
When Tony asked if he could phone his uncle in Seattle.
So Tony's parents answered, "Sure," only to check too late
And find he'd talked from coast-to-coast for fifty minutes straight,
Which started Tony hollering. He wasn't fresh or bad,
He'd asked to call Seattle, and they let him, and he had!

Tony's in the corner upon the Naughty Stool.
All because he tried to do the work in nursery school.
When Tony tired of coloring, to vary his routine
Miss Keith, his teacher, had him make a bowl of plasticine.
But even though he made the bowl, Miss Keith looked fierce and smitten
To note that on the bottom of it MADE IN JAPAN was written!
And since it didn't seem to help when Tony told Miss Keith
He only wrote what all cheap bowls had written underneath . . .

Not really liking fierceness much, he took a pencil WHOOM
And fired it in a rubber band across the silent room.

So Tony's in the corner where he's been sent again
Because — at four — he reads and writes like someone nine or ten.

Upset about the Bowl Affair, Miss Keith — appearing grimmer
Decided Tony might enjoy a lovely first-grade primer.
The trouble was that later on when she was less forbidding
And asked if Tony liked the book, he answered: "Are you kidding?
'My dog can run. My ball is fun. My kitten is a pet.
See Mother cook. See Baby look.' How boring can you get?"
And just to warn some future child the story wasn't bearable,
He scribbled on the title page: "Don't read this book. It's terrible!"
Since Tony, what with this and that, was no example-setter,
The teacher said to stay at home until he acted better,
Which didn't bother Tony much, for what could be forlorner
Than spending half your walking hours restricted to a corner.

So now he's sweeping sidewalks and beating scatter rugs,
And though he keeps his mind alert by watching birds and bugs,
He's sick of how his mother says in accents sad and moany
"He's brilliant, but I don't know what We'll ever do with Tony!"

-The Gifted Pupil
California State Dept. of Ed.
Newsletter. Summer 1977 and
TRIBAL TABLE, Oklahoma MENSA;

21

It is truly sad that the early signs of giftedness in preschoolers are often deliberately slowed down or ignored in order to force the child to conform to more appropriate behaviors. No wonder children learn to be average by fourth grade! Consider the following eight topics concerning the development of preschool gifted children:

1. Being Positive

Parents should avoid direct, indirect, or unspoken attitudes that fantasy, originality, unusual questions, imaginary playmates, or high-level thinking on the part of the children are bad or to be discouraged. Be careful! Laughing at the wrong time can change a child's positive perceptions of himself/herself.

2. Accepting the Mess

Gifted preschoolers like to engage in creative activities that are often messy. The activities must often be left in varying stages of completion. Tolerance and creativity go hand in hand.

3. Worrying

Since gifted preschoolers often have a vague awareness of adult problems, such as

sex, death, illness, war, and finances, which their lack of experience makes them

unable to solve, they need understanding and reassurance on these topics. Talk to them!

4. Solving Problems

Keep out of it! Except in matters of personal safety, do not interfere when your child is trying to solve a problem. Try to help the child discover his/her own solutions to problems. Be available for discussions later.

5. Stimulating

Never stop looking for places to go, things to do, or special lessons to take. You gifted preschooler needs all the "learning by doing" experiences you can provide.

6. Being a Model

Watching someone else having fun learning is contagious. Don't just be a teaching parent, be a learning parent.

7. Conversing

Unfortunately most adults are uncomfortable talking to preschoolers unless they are telling them to do something like "sit down," "hurry up," "wash your hands," or "go to bed." Don't just talk **at** your children, have a conversation **with** them. Little children do have opinions about things. They do have interesting ideas to share.

8. Playing

I wonder how many times in his/her life a child hears an adult say, "Stop playing around. Get to work. Don't play with those things. Pay attention!" Is it any wonder that the word **play** becomes a bad "four-letter word" in the minds of children before they can even talk? Some parents of gifted children regard undirected play as a waste of their youngster's time. Do gifted children waste their time playing? NO. NO. NO. There is more to growing up gifted than reading books and visiting museums. There is play.

WHAT THE EXPERTS HAVE TO SAY ABOUT PLAY

Joseph Pearce, author, parent, and teacher: "Beginning with the first great act of intellect—birth—the human child has only one

concern: to learn all that there is to learn from the world that he/she is part of. This planet is the child's playground and nothing-neither adult values nor concepts of normal growth—should interfere with the child's business to play." *(Magical Child:Rediscovering Nature's Plan for Our Children)*

Fred Rogers, of "Mr. Rogers' Neighborhood," PBS: "Play is a real need for children. It is the most basic means of solving problems and dealing with anxieties. Play may be even more important to the development of gifted and talented kids. So often their abilities tend to make us think they are older and more serious than they really are. It is important that they be given opportunities to be alone

and with peers to engage in play." *(Gifted Children Newsletter,* July, 1981)

Jean Piaget, Swiss biologist turned psychologist: "Play is in the service of intelligence. There are two categories of play in children: fantasy play and imitative play. Play serves many vital needs and functions of the child's growth. However, a child's relentless absorption in play seems to be a problem for adults. Nearly everything we want to do to, with, and even for the child seems to run against this formidable competitor." *(Play, Dreams and Imitation in Childhood)*

Play is absolutely essential in the development of preschool gifted children. It is not purely recreational. Through play, the child has endless opportunities for exploration, open-ended experimentation, discovery through curiosity, and imagination development. Parents should observe their child's play in order to get a better sense of what things interest, excite, or frighten him/her. As a parent, ask yourself, "What is my child trying to tell me through his/her play?" Parents should also set an example as a playful adult. Preschoolers imitate. **Play is a human need not a childhood need.**

HOME ACTIVITIES FOR THE GIFTED PRESCHOOLER

1. Help your child set up a play community using blocks and toy figures, or using boxes and toys. Show how communities are usually organized with certain important services surrounded by neighborhoods or homes.

2. Listen! Explore the sounds of your home and community. Certain jobs make certain sounds (sanitation trucks, police sirens). Try to determine which sound is being heard and discuss the reasons for such loud noises.

3. Discuss your family's cultural heritage with your child. Talk about where his/her ancestors came from. Don't forget to include grandparents.

4. Cook and eat a food from another culture. Talk about the origins of some of the foods you may cook (Italian spaghetti, Mexican tacos). Let the child help prepare the food.

5. Ask at the public library about games from other countries/cultures. Teach your child to play new games that are appropriate for his/her age.

6. Talk with your child about the fruit trees, farm animals, and grain fields from which your food has come at breakfast or another meal. Notice the weather and relate this to good or bad conditions for farming.

7. Help your child recognize the many materials from which clothes are made, such as rubber—boots, gloves; plastic—umbrellas, raincoats, pocketbooks; leather—shoes, belts, billfolds; metal—belts, jewelry; fabric—shirts, pants, dresses; nylon—hose, socks, underwear. The visually impaired or blind child can identify differences by touch.

8. Compare textures and content of fabrics with your child, such as silk, satin, cotton, wool, and synthetic fabrics. Discuss with your child the way clothes are made or acquired. What materials are needed to make clothes? Do some cross-cultural comparisons of clothes.

9. Purchase a pet for your gifted preschooler. Discuss what types of animals make appropriate pets. Develop your child's language and sense of exploration by talking about what his/her pet looks and feels like. Example: "The puppy is as soft as. . . The kitten is as fast as . . ."

10. Ask friends or relatives what pets they have. Ask them to talk to your child about their pet. Take a camera along. Keep a scrapbook of what your child "sees" when he/she is away from home.

11. Talk with your child about extinction and the problem of endangered species. Go to the library and collect more information.

12. Talk about why you go to the doctor and what happens there. There are other people involved in the medical profession also. Physical therapists, nurses, dentists, dieticians, and pharmacists are interesting topics of discussion.

13. Examine some of the instruments used by the doctor or dentist. Talk about their functions and how they will feel when the doctor or dentist uses them.

14. Encourage your child to draw/paint pictures. You make up a story about the picture. Next time, ask the child to make up a story and you draw a picture about it.

15. Provide music for your child in various forms (records, tapes, musical instruments). Talk about different kinds of music, styles, and composers.

16. Memorize a new poem each month. The whole family can participate. Encourage your preschooler to call his/her grandparents and share the poem.

17. Provide several puppets for your children to play with. Encourage them to "talk" for the puppets. Sometimes it is easier for a little child to share his/her feelings through a puppet.

18. Plan and plant a garden with your child. Discuss cost of seed, work involved in weeding, watering, etc.

19. Be a secretary for your preschooler. Write notes and letters to other family members. Encourage your child to share his/her own thoughts and feelings. You do the printing.

20. Do lots of "predicting" activities. Will it be warm or cool tomorrow? How long will it take to drive to the store? How many cookies are in the package?

21. Give your child choices whenever possible. Do you want to go to the playground or the zoo tomorrow? Which should we do first, make the bed or brush our teeth?

22. Ask for your child's opinion. Which one do you like the best? Can you tell me why?

* Adapted from *Planning Guide for Gifted Preschoolers.*

THEY'RE EVERYWHERE! THEY'RE EVERYWHERE!

There are perhaps three to five gifted preschoolers in every 100. Sometimes they jump out at me when I least expect it. How could I ever forget the day, while waiting in a carpeted lounge area in a major airport, the three-year-old girl who proclaimed in a very loud voice to her parents and me, "Look at the floor! Look at the floor! There are hexagons and pentagons in the design. Just like at Aunt Betty's!" Or the time Stevie, my godchild, asked, "Aunt Nancy, ya know what they call a house where nobody lives? A motel!" Yes, they are everywhere, these children of promise. Little people with a potential so big that it frightens most of us. If you have the privilege to know one, be glad and proud. If you haven't met a gifted preschooler yet, you have only to listen, to look around, to pay attention. The Tonys, the Suzies, and the Stevies are all out there waiting to be discovered and enjoyed.

RESOURCES

Clark, Barbara. *Growing Up Gifted.* Columbus, OH: Charles Merrill Publishing Company, 1979.

Leonard, Judith et al. *Planning Guide for Gifted Preschoolers.* Winston-Salem, NC: Kaplan Press.

Moore, Linda Perigo. *Does This Mean My Kid's a Genius?* New York: McGraw Hill Book Company, 1981.

Pearce, Joseph Chilton. *Magical Child.* New York: E.P. Dutton, 1977.

Perino, Sheila, and Joseph Perino. *Parenting the Gifted: Developing the Promise.* New York: Bowker Company, 1981.

Piaget, Jean. *Play, Dreams and Imitation in Childhood.* New York: W.W. Norton & Company, 1962.

Roedell, Windy Conklin, Nancy E. Jackson, and Halbert B. Robinson. *Gifted Young Children.* New York: Teachers College Press, 1980.

Webb, James T., Elizabeth Meckstroth, and Stephanie Tolan. *Guiding the Gifted Child.* Columbus, OH: Ohio Psychology Publishing Co.mpany, 1982.

YOUR GIFTED DAUGHTER

What Is She Really Made Of?

There is an old-fashioned rhyme that says something about little boys being made of snakes and snails and puppy dog tails and little girls of sugar and spice and everything nice. Such a definition seems rather simplistic for today's sophisticated, fast-paced society. However, the word "spice" may just be what we are looking for when the little girl in question happens to be gifted.

Just as we enjoy spices in several flavors, textures, and aromas, from clove and cinnamon to nutmeg and pepper, so it is with gifted girls. They come in various sizes, shapes, and colors and possess a variety of fascinating and diverse personality traits.

Many are nonstop talkers with energy levels to match. Most have at least one gifted parent. They have high levels of curiosity about objects, ideas, situations, or events. Many mature physically one to two years before their peers. They typically learn to read earlier, with a better comprehension of the nuances of the language. Most gifted girls exhibit an intrinsic motivation to learn and explore; they are highly inquisitive and very persistent. Many are less inhibited than their peers in expressing opinions and ideas. They often display intellectual playfulness, fantasize, and imagine readily.

Of course, many of the characteristics of gifted girls are also applicable to gifted boys. The research on the intellectual abilities of gifted females as compared to gifted males is inconclusive. One exception might be in the area of mathematics where there is a much higher proportion of males identified as gifted.

One of the best ways to find out what gifted girls are really made of is to explore the lives of famous gifted women past and present. The "spice" to be found in these women should be an inspiration and source of pride for all present, as well as future, generations of gifted girls. Unfortunately, society has been slow in recognizing many gifted women who have contributed immeasurably to the development of society. In many instances, textbook historians have overlooked some incredibly gifted women.

STEPHANIE KWOLEK, chemist: In 1965, Stephanie made the pioneering chemical discovery that led to the development of the material in bulletproof vests. "I love the challenge and the research," she says. "You need tremendous drive to remain in this line of work. It's hard to believe that it's taken such a long time for women to be recognized as scientists. The abilities have been there all along." Stephanie holds a total of fifteen U.S. patents. ("Fifty American Heroines," *Ladies Home Journal,* July, 1984)

EMMA WILLIARD, educator: In 1804, Emma was denied permission to enter the University of Middleburg. She was not even allowed to take the entrance examinations. At that time, it was thought that universities and higher education were for men only. Many believed that women's brains were smaller and inferior to those of men. Education for women at that time was domestic education. However, Emma studied to develop her own methods of teaching and learning and ultimately founded her own school, the Troy Female Seminary. One of the courses taught at her school was physiology, a course considered quite inappropriate and improper for women. (B. McDowell and J. Umlaug, editors, *Woman's Almanac.* New York: Newspaper Enterprise Association Inc., 1977)

TERESA DE CEPEDA Y AHUMEDA, writer and church reformer: Teresa of Avila, a canonized saint of the Roman Catholic Church and a famous Christian mystic, was a woman of genius and courage. She was born in the Castillian town of Avila, Spain, on March 28, 1515. The mental abilities of this incredible woman were revealed in her writings, which include four books, several minor pieces, and prolific correspondence, giving Spanish literature its sole female genius. As a woman of action, she faced the dangers of

angry churchmen who opposed her plan to reform the Carmelite Order. However, Teresa lived long enough to see the Reformed Order of Carmelite Friars and Nuns organized independently from any authority in Spain. She is acknowledged as one of Spain's greatest women. (Elaine Crocitz and Elizabeth Buford, *Courage Knows No Sex*. North Quincy, MA: The Christopher Publishing House, 1978)

MERCY OTIS WARREN, poet, satirist, dramatist, and historian: A late bloomer who was not known to the public until she was in her forties, Mercy has been called the "first lady of the American Revolution." In 1772, she began to engage actively in the political debates that led to the war with England. Much of Mercy's impact on the thinking of her fellow colonists can be attributed to her intelligence and political acumen. Members of her own family have described her as a brainy adolescent, tender wife, powerful mother, ardent propagandist, fiery crusader, defiant adult, political theorist, loving woman, sharp-tongued conversationalist, and multi-faceted historical writer. (*Courage Knows No Sex*)

RENEE POUSSAINT, TV anchorwoman: Renee has had to fight double stereotypes, both as a black and as a woman in order to get her position. She was once told by a male television executive, "News coming from a woman's mouth sounds like gossip. And that's why there are no women anchors at this station." Another time she was told that she would never be a successful anchor because she was too intelligent on the air and that viewers resented intelligence. Renee plans to move into TV management because she feels

that the media industry will not change enough until more blacks and women are in decision-making positions. (L. Berger, *The Washington Post,* February 9, 1982)

There are more gifted women, of course, buried in dusty history books, family trees, historical society records, the minds and memories of our great-grandmothers, and even in obscure corners of today's newspapers. All of them important. All of them are strong, courageous women. Full of "spice"! All of them are capable of being a role model or heroine for your gifted daughter.

FROM THE PAST

Elizabeth Blackwell of Geneva, New York, became the first U.S. woman doctor in 1848.

Frances Perkins was the first woman named to the U.S. Cabinet as Secretary of Labor in 1933.

Mary Anderson invented the windshield wiper in 1902 and received a patent for her invention that same year.

Annie J. Cannon was an astronomer who discovered more than 5,000 stars during her forty years as a researcher at Harvard University.

FROM THE PRESENT

Janie Shores was the first woman to ever sit on the Alabama Supreme Court. She was elected to her seat in 1974 with the largest vote ever. From her position, she fought sexual discrimination against women and men. Fathers can now gain custody of their young children, and a woman no longer needs her husband's consent to sell their property.

Melanie Chang formed a travel service in 1978 that enabled handicapped people to enjoy the wonders of her home state of Hawaii. She also founded the Disabled Sports Association, which puts on clinics and meets for people with a variety of disabilities.

Sandra Day O'Connor was the first woman on the U.S. Supreme Court. She graduated first in her class at Stanford Law School in 1952.

Is it feminine to be smart? Is it smart to be feminine? The word is androgynous. The gifted girl needs help and support to develop and maintain a COMBINATION of traditional masculine and feminine traits. She must understand the stereotypes that may pressure her to exhibit only feminine traits.

SEX ROLE STEREOTYPES

MASCULINE	FEMININE	NEUTRAL
aggressive	sympathetic	conceited
ambitious	tender	truthful
dominant	shy	friendly
assertive	gullible	sincere
athletic	yielding	helpful
competitive	soft-spoken	jealous
leader	easy to flatter	reliable
individualistic	love for kids	conventional
analytical	loyal	adaptable

*Bem Sex Role Inventory (Bem & Bem, 1972)

STRATEGIES FOR RAISING A GIFTED DAUGHTER

Teach the importance of independence. Try NOT to be an overprotective parent. Independence raises self-esteem; dependence inhibits it. Allow your daughter to get herself in and out of trouble. Be supportive, but do not "rescue" her. When she is permitted to experience the consequences of her own behavior, she will have the opportunity to learn from her mistakes.

Encourage your gifted daughter to get involved in a variety of experiences. The process of planning, setting goals, and completing products/projects should be stressed. Lots of positive reinforcement is in order! The development of leadership skills begins with small steps; i.e., part-time job, president of student council, captain of the volleyball team. Beware! Traditional feminine roles may limit your daughter's opportunities. Be there to help her open some new doors!

Help your daughter to be nonjudgmental. Listen for derogatory statements from your daughter. Being critical and prejudiced comes from a need to make others look inferior, small, or less important in order to feel better about oneself. Talk about it. Being gifted means you are different from, not better than, others.

Discuss success and failure. Encourage your daughter to become a risk taker. In order for her to make the fullest possible use of her abilities, your daughter must develop the skills of self-evaluation. Remember, failure doesn't mean failure as a person. Be a model. When was the last time you tried something and then failed? A gifted girl is less likely than a gifted boy to attribute success to her own ability, and she will often internalize failures. Encourage your daughter to incorporate more positive attitudes into her thoughts and speech.

Reduce the emphasis on material rewards. A positive self-concept means more than straight A's, trophies, and first-place finishes. If your daughter can have a real feeling of accomplishment without a gold star, she is learning the first steps of real success and self-worth. However, our society quite often devalues the achievements of females because of the limited definition of competence for women. Consequently, it is sometimes difficult for gifted girls to really feel good and not feel guilty about their accomplishments.

Discuss the various life styles and career choices that are open to women. Your daughter needs to explore, with your encouragement, the many options available to her. Will she go to college? If so, will her future beyond college be determined by marriage and family issues? Can she have a career and family? Should she marry? What if she doesn't? What if a marriage fails? Will she be able to support herself emotionally and financially? Should she have a family first and then a career? Or a career first? Or both? Talk about it. Your gifted daughter has extraordinary abilities. Along with those abilities come some very difficult problems and choices. The life-style she chooses will determine whether or not her gifts and talents are developed to their fullest. Her career goals should be commensurate with her abilities.

Investigate all the possibilities the elementary/secondary schools have to offer your gifted daughter. Find out what is or isn't happening for gifted children in your school and/or state. Do gifted girls have the same opportunities as gifted boys? Are certain academic activities denied your daughter just because she is a female? Are guidance personnel available to counsel gifted students?

"No one can make you feel inferior without your consent." (Eleanor Roosevelt)

"Far away, there in the sunshine are my highest aspirations. I may not reach them, but I can look up and see their beauty, believe in them, and try to follow where they lead." (Louisa May Alcott)

"I have always been glad that I was born a girl." (Margaret Mead)

"Don't despair, young women. When you feel low pray to God. SHE will help us all." (Susan B. Anthony)

30

Underneath It All . .

Underneath the sugar and the spice
Are snakes and snails and puppy dog tails.
Underneath the sugar and the spice
Are potentialities and paradoxes.
Underneath the sugar and spice are:
Hair ribbons and blue jeans
Brains and bubble gum
Mud pies and lace
Dolls and computers
Guitars and crescent wrenches
Uniforms and diapers
Slide rules and satin
Lipstick and spaceships
Finish lines and chorus lines.
Underneath it all is true femininity.
Underneath it all is pride.
Pride in being a human being who happens to be female.
Pride in being a female who happens to be gifted,
And the courage to be all three.

    – NLJ

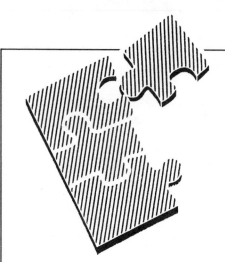

IS THIS CHILD GIFTED?

The Gifted/Learning Disabled Child: Reshaping the Puzzle

Dear, Mrs. melton

By now, Randles probably brought you the plack we youre fiftgrade math/science class wished you to have as a tocen of are appreciation For The Things you did For us in The Last Few years. it will be hard aT First to adjust to The middle shcoole but ones they instal the program, That is IF They do! Things will ashuridly improve. And I would Like To Show my concern about your Father I can understand the greef you must have suferd. but NOW I would Like to ask if "as soon as you have the chance" To Send me ineny way conveniant to you my Star wars book. I was meaning To bring it home but we were so beasy it sliped my mind, and I mite say it's just my luck we came within a days work of completing that project "that is if I would alow myself to believe in such things as LUck" and sence I've forgoten the moral of this Letter. I'd better sighn of but before I do I just want to Say That I've Truly injoyed working with you These Last Two years, and iF you need the apenule of a Formor Student please don't hesatate best of Luck!

Sincerely yours

. . . a special letter, to a special teacher, written by a very special young man. Is this child learning disabled? Yes. He suffers from dyslexia. Is this child gifted? Yes. The insight, humor, and sensitivity he expresses in this letter match the opinions of his teacher that he is an exceptional child. Is he currently involved in a gifted program? No. WHY?

The problem is a tough one. Like pieces of a jigsaw puzzle, some seem to slide into place with ease, while others defy every effort to make them fit. Two of the most puzzling pieces might be labeled "gifted" and "learning disabled." As long as these two pieces do not have to fit together, the problem of finding their proper places in the puzzle is easy. Each has its own separate space to fill. But when the two pieces must fit together, side-by-side, interlocking and dependent, only the most patient and caring problem solver will find a solution.

Even the sound of the language—gifted/learning disabled, gifted/learning disabled, gifted/learning disabled—seems like a contradiction in terms. However, as strange as the label sounds and as unusual as the puzzle pieces appear, it is time to face the reality of the gifted/learning disabled child. Perhaps a closer look at each piece will result in a reshaping of opinions and ideas and thereby force the reshaping, not of the pieces, but of the puzzle itself.

DEFINING THE PIECES

It would be presumptuous and inaccurate to say that educators know precisely what giftedness is and what learning disability is. Certainly more is known today than 50 years ago. But one has only to attend a regional or national conference on gifted education or learning disabilities and eavesdrop on conversations to learn that the state of the art in identification has yet to be reached. In the face of such controversy, one usually reverts to old methods and ideas, even though they might be flawed.

Gifted Children. As stated in Chapter 2, the U.S. Office of Education, under the directive of Public Law 91-230, Section 806, has established the following definition: "Gifted and talented children are those identified by professionally qualified persons who by virtue of outstanding abilities are capable of high performance. These children require differentiated educational programs and/or services beyond those normally provided by the regular school program in order to realize their contribution to self and society. Children capable of high performance include those with demonstrated achievement and/or potential ability in any of the following areas, singly or in combination: general intellectual ability, leadership, specific academic aptitude, visual and performing arts, creative thinking, and psychomotor ability. It can be assumed that utilization of these criteria for identification of the gifted and talented will encompass a minimum of three to five percent of the school population."

Learning Disabilities. The U.S. Office of Education, under the directive of Public Law 94-142, has established the following definition: "Specific learning disability means a disorder in one or more of the basic psychological processes involved in understanding or in using language, spoken or written, which may manifest itself in an imperfect ability to listen, think, speak, read, write, spell, or do mathematical calculations. The term includes such conditions as perceptual handicaps, brain injury, minimal brain dysfunction, dyslexia, and developmental aphasia. The term does **not** include children who have learning problems which are primarily the result of visual, hearing, or motor handicaps, of mental retardation, of emotional disturbance, or of environmental, cultural, or economic disadvantage."

An educator or parent who notices a bright, intellectually endowed child who is **not** academically successful and who demonstrates three of the following traits probably has discovered a gifted child who is learning disabled (Daniels, *Teaching the Gifted/Learning Disabled Child*, see bibliography).

● **"They find it difficult to react to situations that differ from their perceived routines."**

Gifted/learning disabled children often have difficulty adapting to new situations. When forced to adapt, they quite often lock up and become rigid. To many of these children, life is a game that they must play, and the rules are constantly changing. They do not feel in control and often complain about being manipulated by parents, teachers, and other children. They express a "What's the use?" attitude. This air of hopelessness usually results in yet another label for these children: UNMOTIVATED.

● **"They tend to be rigid and nonflexible in their approaches to problems."**

Gifted/learning disabled children would like to live in a world which has one set of rules that never changes. To even suggest to these children that there might be more than one answer to a given question results in anxiety. When flexibility (an expected characteristic of gifted children) begins to destroy their structured world, gifted/learning disabled children succumb to panic accompanied by a helpless attitude.

● **"They lack speed of reaction, especially in language areas."**

Many gifted/learning disabled children tend to be slow and plodding in their reaction time, especially in testing situations. Since nearly all standardized tests are timed, children who work slowly tend to be penalized. The overall scores of gifted/learning disabled children may **not** reflect their true capabilities.

- **"They lack vocabulary sophistication and appreciation."**

Gifted/learning disabled children do not seem to have any difficulty in acquiring vocabulary. They might even perform better than their age peers. However, they do not readily participate in activities that might **broaden** their language base. They will read all they can get their hands on about a certain topic and refuse to read anything else.

Comments from parents and educators concerning gifted/learning disabled children include:

- His organizational skills are terrible.
- She has the messiest locker in the school!
- Behavior modification seems to work well.
- He denies that he even has a problem.
- Her behavior is either passive or aggressive.
- She needs constant motivation to get things done.
- He just can't seem to separate the wheat from the chaff when learning.
- He needs peace and quiet to get things done.
- Her figure /ground strengths need work.
- He needs more structure and routine.

- Sometimes this child is the brightest and dumbest child I know!
- He tries to use his greater intelligence to not solve problems.
- She is a physical/visual learner rather than oral.
- She is slow when taking tests.
- He will skip steps and jump forward when solving problems.
- She has sequencing problems.
- He seems to be externally oriented, not introspective.
- He has difficulty in relating to the abstract.
- He is a whiz in math or reading but not in both.
- She expects adults to solve all problems for her.

Parents: "It's all the school's fault!"

Educators: "It's the home situation!"

Child: "It's my fault. I can't do anything right!"

Voice of Truth: "Aren't we all in this together?"

The most important thing to remember concerning the identification of these very special children is not to overlook either the giftedness or the learning disability. We have a tendency to focus on one or the other. The recognition of giftedness overshadows the recognition of the learning disability OR the recognition of the learning disability over shadows the recognition of giftedness. Either way, the oversight means we are not considering the whole child. What we end up with is a child who cannot function in a "regular" gifted program because he/she has

an undetected learning disability AND a child who cannot function in a regular learning disabilities class because it is a remedial program that does not meet the high intellectual needs of the gifted. Is it any wonder, as Daniels says, "that feelings of defectiveness and despair are the end products of such well-intentioned **but unsuitable programs.**"

SUGGESTIONS FOR ADMINISTRATORS

1. Allow teachers to use materials and equipment other than those designated for specific grade level.

2. Support and encourage teachers who attend special classes and/or workshops concerning gifted/learning disabled children.

3. Be as flexible as possible in changing the schedule to allow larger blocks of time for teachers to work with gifted/learning disabled children.

4. Allow teachers to report to parents concerning student progress in ways other than grades (criterion-referenced inventories).

5. The teacher of the gifted, remedial teacher, learning disabilities teacher, classroom teacher, and parents should be required to plan **together** for the needs of the gifted/learning disabled child. Time must be provided for them to do such planning.

6. Accept the responsibility for public relations. The public, which includes the school board and parents, must be educated to understand the meanings of giftedness and learning disability.

SUGGESTIONS FOR TEACHERS AND PARENTS

1. Use clear stencils and dittos. Fuzzy, purple print creates fear in the hearts of gifted/learning disabled children!

2. Ask the children how you can help them. Remember, these are bright children who may have insight into their own learning problems.

3. Test/teach/test/teach/test/teach/test—evaluation becomes a crucial teaching tool when dealing with gifted/learning disabled children. Make no assumptions about what they know!

4. Encourage and teach the application of what is learned, as well as problem solving, independent learning, and thinking skills. Help the children to become more inner directed, rather than outer directed and dependent.

5. Provide lots of adaptive learning materials. Raid the supply room and learning center/library for hand calculators, typewriters, tape recorders, language masters, chalkboards, and overhead projectors. And don't forget computers. Next to teachers and parents, the computer may be the best teaching tool available to gifted/learning disabled children.

6. Work constantly on improving communication through talking, telephoning, notes, and letters.

7. Try to improve the children's self-esteem. Fighting that worthless/useless attitude is a constant battle. Have evidence on hand of past successes and documented evidence of progress. Be sure and share this evidence with the gifted/learning disabled children.

8. Discuss positive and negative attention with the children. Quite often gifted/learning disabled children do not know the difference.

9. Develop responsibilities at home as well as in school. Don't use responsibilities as a punishment for bad behavior. Example: "If you don't stop that, you will have to clean your room five times next week!"

10. Maintain an attitude that says, "I won't give up on you!"

I wish I had more suggestions.

I wish there were easy answers.

I wish the pieces would quickly slide into place everytime I pick one up.

I wish we had more teachers like Shirley Melton who considers it a privilege to have taught the child who wrote the letter and is grateful that he continues to communicate with her.

I wish the paradox that allows certain educators to state that gifted/learning disabled children, by definition, cannot exist was against the law.

I wish parents understood that each child is different and unique and therefore should not always be treated the same.

I wish gifted/learning disabled children would never accept their disabilities and turn them into handicaps they must suffer with forever.

I wish Buckminster Fuller were still alive to remind us that it is possible to learn and not understand, to know and not be able to do.

I have the pieces.

I wish I had a new puzzle.

RESOURCES

Badian, N.A, and M. Ghublikian. "The Personal —Social—Characteristics of Children with Poor Mathematical Computation Skills." *Journal of Learning Disabilities.* March, 1983.

Daniels, P.R. *Teaching the Gifted/Learning Disabled Child.* Rockville, MD: Aspen Publications, 1983.

Dunn, R.K. "Learning Style and Its Relation to Exceptionality at Both Ends of the Spectrum." *Exceptional Children.* April, 1983.

French, J.M. "The Gifted Learning Disabled Child." *Roeper Review.* 1982.

Whitmore, J.R. *Giftedness, Conflict and Underachievement.* Boston: Allyn and Bacon, Inc., 1980.

Foundation for Children with Learning Disabilities, Box 2929 Grand Central Station New York, NY 10163

A Special Note:

The author would like to extend her personal thanks to Mrs. Shirley A. Melton, teacher of the gifted in Harrah, Oklahoma, for sharing the letter that introduces this article. And a very special thank you to the young man and his parents who agreed to the letter's publication. Perhaps your kindness and courage will help shape the puzzle for some other child.

A Guide To Right/Left Hemisphere Functions

Part I

THE SCENE: A telephone conversation between the parents of two gifted children.

THE TIME: The evening following a parent/teacher conference.

Mrs. Smith: "Hello, Martha. This is Virginia. I just came from school and a conference with Becky's teacher. He said she is a right-brained child who has a metaphoric, spatial, and holistic nature. Does that mean anything to you, Martha? What do you suppose he meant by that?"

Mrs. Brown: "Gee, Virginia, it sounds like your Becky has only half a brain. Don't worry; she probably inherited it from George's side of the family!"

Mrs. Smith: "He also talked about her right hemisphere and left hemisphere. Does that sound familiar to you, Martha?"

Mrs. Brown: "Hmmmm, Virginia, are you sure he said right and left hemispheres? Maybe he meant north and south hemispheres. Sounds to me like your Becky is having trouble in geography!"

Yes, Virginia, Becky **does** have a right hemisphere and left hemisphere. No, Martha, she is not having trouble in geography, and she **does not** have half a brain. Parents all over the country are hearing a new language from educators concerning their child's learning style and thinking skills. More and more teachers are becoming aware of the research concerning left-brain/right-brain function. This awareness quickly turns to excitement because, for the first time, teachers have some answers to previously unexplained abilities, behaviors, and problems in their students. . . And if the information will help teachers become better teachers, perhaps it will help parents become better parents. In either case, the ones who benefit most will be the children.

It has been known for some time that the human brain is divided into two sides, or hemispheres. More nerve connections exist between these halves of the brain than from the brain to the rest of the body. This makes the human brain a very expensive organ, demanding more energy to function properly than any other organ of the body.

The left hemisphere is most responsible for rational, logical, sequential, linear, and abstract thinking. Among other things, the left brain unlocks and decodes words. Our language is stored in that side of the brain, and as we speak, we "pull" words out of the left side of our head. The right hemisphere is responsible for a different kind of thinking that is equally important.

The right side seems to be intuitive, spatial, visual, and concrete. It is from this side of the brain that we are able to visualize. The right brain can make the printed word "come alive" by creating pictures or images in the mind about the characters, places, and things described in print.

The following list of left-brain/right-brain functions will explain the differences in the two hemispheres.

LEFT-BRAIN FUNCTIONS

critical thinking
sequential thinking
logical thinking
analysis
evaluative thinking
convergent thinking
focal thinking
sees parts/segments
linear functions
verbal
verbal instructions
controlled experimenting
serious ideas/logical ideas
math (algebra)
objective processing of ideas
dislikes improvisation
little use of metaphors
little use of analogies
receptive
abstract math computation
sequencing of concepts
verbal memory
reading/phonics
writing
ordering/sequencing
planning
verifying
duplication and application
reality
improving known
nonfiction
interpreting behavior

RIGHT-BRAIN FUNCTIONS

creative thinking/synthesis
simultaneity
intuitive thinking
visual analysis
evaluative thinking
divergent thinking
diffuse thinking
sees holistically/Gestalten
nonlinear functions
visual/spatial
visual/kinesthetic instructions
playful/loose experimenting
humorous ideas
math (geometry)
subjective processing of ideas
likes improvisation
use of metaphors
use of analogies
self-acting
simple math computation
relational concepts
tonal memory
sight reading
singing
random exploration
dreaming
assuming
imagination
fantasy
inventing
fiction
affective interaction

Did you read the left-brain list carefully? What you are looking at is the American school system. Most of the learning experiences that take place in the regular classrooms of this country involve left-brain functions. Schools have concentrated their efforts on the cognitive, left-brain type of learning, while DEVALUING the creative right-brain experiences. To reach an individual's full potential, he/she must experience both left- and right-brain functions. When only the rational, cognitive functions are used, we paradoxically limit those functions. And without the support and integration of a well-developed right hemisphere, the growth of the left hemisphere is inhibited.

The constant interaction and intersupport between the two hemispheres does not occur exactly the same way in all people. Dr. Jerry Levy in her research on brain development, refers to differing arousal levels between the right and left brain. For example, the left hemisphere in one person may possess a very high arousal level, while the left hemisphere in another person may be much lower. A person with a high arousal level in his/her left brain may appear extremely logical or practical in decision making. He/She would be very organized, punctual, and would get upset if things did not go as planned.

On the other hand, some people may have a very high arousal level in their right brain. Such people tend to be flexible thinkers, creative, and somewhat disorganized. They usually have their own concept of time and have a strong dislike for details.

A high arousal level or strength in a child's left or right brain can affect the way he/she lives, learns, and relates to people. Does your gifted child have a particularly strong left or right brain? Read the following list of characteristics for left- and right-brained people. Try to relate the characteristics to your gifted child, other family members, and yourself.

LEFT-BRAIN CHARACTERISTICS

____ Is good at remembering names.

____ Will answer best to directions which are spoken or written down.

____ Likes to keep things to himself/herself.

____ When trying something new, he/she always likes to think through alternatives before he/she makes an attempt.

____ Likes to do things one at a time.

____ Likes tests where the answers are given and he/she must pick the best one (multiple choice, true/false).

____ Waits for people to tell him/her when they are happy or sad.

____ Is not good at thinking up funny things to say and do (serious attitude about things).

____ Is time conscious, likes meetings to start and end on time (feels "naked" without a wristwatch).

____ Likes agendas, program booklets, outlines, lists, written contracts, and agreements.

____ Likes neatness in self and others.

____ Has a fairly long attention span, is a good listener, and is able to concentrate on one subject for a long period of time.

____ Is not a risk taker, is careful, does not like to make mistakes, and is a perfectionist.

____ Likes to follow numbered written directions.

____ Will ask many questions before making a decision and is stubborn and overly cautious when placed in a problem-solving situation.

____ Likes to read (the book is always better than the movie).

39

RIGHT-BRAIN CHARACTERISTICS

____ Is good at remembering faces.

____ Will answer best to directions which are shown or demonstrated.

____ Likes to let people know how he/she feels.

____ Likes to try things that he/she has not tried before.

____ Likes to do several things at once.

____ Likes tests where he/she writes out the answer (essay).

____ Can tell when someone is happy or not without the person telling him/her.

____ Is good at thinking of funny things to say and do (class clown).

____ Is a random learner, shows up late for meetings, and seems to have his/her own concept of time.

____ Dislikes structured situations, details, and agendas.

____ Has a high tolerance for clutter, and is disorganized and messy.

____ Has a short attention span, is "spacy," and a daydreamer whose mind wanders a lot.

____ Is a risk taker and does not always fear failure.

____ Dislikes written directions and likes to picture the answer to a problem in his/her head.

____ Likes to guess at the answer or use intuition in problem-solving situations.

____ Likes to draw.

____ Will use anything around to get things done.

____ Uses a "jam-it-and-cram-it" system of organization.

So are you living with a "right-brainder" or "left-brainder"? You may have identified some characteristics from both lists.

REMEMBER:

● No one is totally left- or right-brained. We all use both sides of our brains to think. However, many people exhibit behaviors that indicate a preference for one side over the other. That is, one of the two hemispheres is dominant in terms of our preferred mode of processing information. The two hemispheres work together, but one clearly takes the lead.

● There are degrees or levels of right-brain or left-brain thinking. For example, the right-brain arousal in one person might be very high. Such a person would exhibit at least 15 of the right-brain characteristics. Another right-brained person with a lower right-brain arousal level might exhibit only 12 of the charac-

teristics. However, both could still be labeled "right-brainders."

- Children with strong right-brain characteristics are at a distinct disadvantage in our schools. They must learn to survive in a society that admires, rewards, and generally caters to left-brain behavior. Gifted programs quite often fail to identify a gifted child because of his/her right-brain behavior. Educators and/or parents must STOP trying to change a right-brained child's thinking preference and START accepting him/her as a unique individual.

- Accepting a child's thinking and learning preference is crucial if he/she is to develop into a happy, healthy, functioning human being. It is up to parents and educators to let the child with strong left- or right-brain tendencies know that it is OK. The child's positive self-concept depends on it.

- To reach an individual's full potential, he/she must experience BOTH left- and right-brain functions. Therefore, it is important to "stretch" the right-brained child into using his/her left brain and the left-brained child into using his/her right brain.

RESOURCES

Well, do you have questions? The bad news is that all the research is not complete, and some that has been done is not conclusive. The good news is that there are many researchers still working on the unanswered questions. In the meantime, the best advice is to attend an educator's workshop on left/right-brain thinking and read some of the following resources:

Buzan, Tony. *Using Both Sides of Your Brain*. New York: E.P. Dutton, 1974.

Coulter, D.J. "New Paradigms for Understanding the Properties and Functions of the Brain: Implications for Education" (A research project). Greeley, CO: University of Northern Colorado, 1981.

Edwards, Betty. *Drawing on the Right Side of the Brain*. Los Angeles: J.T. Tarcher, 1979.

Epstein, H.T. *Education and the Brain*. Chicago: University of Chicago Press, 1970.

Wayman, Joseph. *The Other Side of Reading: The Forgotten Skills*. Carthage, IL: Good Apple, Inc., 1979.

The left-right brain functions list was adapted from Dr. Paul Torrance and Dr. Bernice McCarthy, 1979.

A BRAIN DIVIDED: Part II

In the first part of this chapter we explored some of the latest research concerning right- and left-brain functions. Among other things, we learned that the left hemisphere is most responsible for rational, logical, sequential, linear, and abstract thinking. Some of the characteristics of the left brain include: (1) likes to do things one at a time, (2) will answer best to directions which are spoken or written, and (3) is not a risk taker, is careful, does not like to make mistakes, and is a perfectionist. In addition, a person with a high arousal level in his/her left brain might appear extremely logical or practical in decision making. He/She is very organized, punctual, and tends to get upset if things do not go as planned.

The right hemisphere is responsible for a different kind of thinking that is equally important. The right side seems to be intuitive, spatial, visual, and concrete. Some characteristics of the right brain include: (1) likes to do several things at once, (2) likes to guess at the answer or use intuition in problem solving, and (3) will answer best to directions which are shown or demonstrated. In addition, a person with a high arousal level in his/her right brain tends to be a flexible thinker, creative, and somewhat disorganized. He/She usually has his/her own concept of time and tends to have a strong dislike for details.

After exploring some of the facts that the research has to offer, many times the reader is left with a "So what?" attitude. Applying the research on a personal, practical level is probably the most exciting and important part of the learning process. So here is . . .

THE REST OF THE STORY:

THE SCENE: A telephone conversation between the parents of two gifted children.

THE TIME: About two months ago.

Mrs. Smith: "Hello, Martha. This is Virginia. Did you read **THE Faces OF Gifted** ? There is an article in it about that left and right-hemisphere stuff that Becky's teacher was telling me about."

Mrs. Brown: "I'm way ahead of you, Virginia. I've already sent the book to Billy's teacher. The section describing left-brained thinking really fits our Billy, especially the part about being a perfectionist."

Mrs. Smith: "Well, our Becky is just the opposite. She came up right-brained on that checklist."

Mrs. Brown: "Isn't it amazing that our kids can be so different and still be considered gifted?"

Mrs. Smith: "Well, amazing or not, Martha, they are kids. And left hemisphere or right hemisphere, gifted or not, there are times when Billy drives us crazy!"

Yes, Virginia, ACCEPTING a child's thinking and learning preferences is sometimes difficult, but it is crucial if he/she is to develop into a happy, healthy, functioning person. Unfortunately, we live in a society that does not value differences. As parents and teachers, we need to help our gifted children ACCEPT themselves as they are, and at the same time, encourage them to STRETCH their thinking and learning abilities. Stretching both sides of the brain is important if an individual is to reach his/her full potential. The following suggestions, using Billy and Becky as examples, are offered in an effort to speed up this progress of accepting and stretching your left-brained or right-brained child.

ganizing family trips. He loves it and does it well. His dad can't wait until Billy is old enough to manage the family budget! His parents are especially aware of Billy's constant need for praise and reinforcement. Nothing brings a smile to his face quicker than a "Good for you, Billy. You did a fine job!"

Billy is a collector—an organized collector. Each treasure has its own place in his room. His mom saves all types of containers (shoe boxes, jars, sacks, etc.) for him to use to organize his "stuff." However, when it comes to clothes, he needs some extra help from other family members. He doesn't always choose outfits that "go together." He will wear his favorite shirt and favorite pants unaware that a red and yellow-dotted shirt and purple and gray-striped pants visually clash. Billy looks at himself and his world in segments or pieces. He sees the trees but not the forest. He doesn't always see the whole picture; he sees individual parts. And the result sometimes is two parts that don't fit the whole, for example, the striped pants and dotted shirt. So, nobody in the family laughs when Billy models an outfit and asks, "Does this look OK? I can't tell." A seemingly unlikely question from a child with an IQ of 140.

ACCEPTING BILLY'S LEADING LEFT BRAIN

Billy is a perfectionist. As far as Billy is concerned, there is a right way and a wrong way to do things. His parents know that Billy will need a little extra time to complete tasks. Their patience will allow him to "do the job right." Whenever possible, family chores and activities are discussed well in advance and then written on a calendar for all to see, especially Billy. He likes to know what's going to happen and when. Planning and discussion take time. (Billy will ask 100 questions!) However, his parents know that in the long run, it is time well spent. There will be much less stress on their son if he isn't "kept in the dark" about things. Sometimes Billy is given sole responsibility for planning and or-

More than anything else, Billy is a voracious reader. He loves to learn by reading, not by doing. He is the proud possessor of not one

but three library cards. (His parents worked for weeks to get the one from the state library.)

Billy's birthday is coming up. He wants a watch that tells the date, the time in four countries, chimes on the hour, has a stop-watch button, and plays three tunes. A super gift idea for a time-conscious, left-brained child!

STRETCHING BILLY'S RIGHT BRAIN

To sharpen Billy's visual skills and make him more aware of the forest, not the trees, his parents purchased a 35mm camera and enrolled him in a photography class at the local junior college. Of course, at first, Billy was more interested in how the camera worked instead of what you could see with it!

Billy's flexible thinking abilities will be improved if he is living in a more flexible environment. So, every few weeks, the furniture in various rooms of the house is rearranged. Billy is not always pleased about his room being changed, but his tolerance for

it has certainly improved. (Stretching takes time and patience.)

One of the toughest stretching experiences for Billy is risk taking. Trying and failing is really traumatic for him. His parents have learned that the best way to encourage their son to take risks is to be model risk takers themselves. Billy is learning through example that "messing up" is not fatal, that learning by doing can be fun, and that nobody is perfect.

Finally, sometimes, it's the little things that count. Here are some suggestions that might seem insignificant individually but when combined will help Billy to be less structured in his thinking and behavior.

- Practice traveling to school, church, or the store using a different route or a different mode of transportation.

- Use round tables instead of square ones especially for the family dining table.

- Add artwork to the living environment. (paintings, sculpture, weaving.)

- Play the "What if . . . Game" while riding in the car. Example: What if all the water in the world turned to soda pop? What would happen? Stress the importance of no right or wrong answers, just lots of possibilities!

- Change or restructure some family living patterns. Have an indoor picnic and eat dinner on the floor in one family member's bedroom. Eat dinner backwards, with dessert first. Have a "green dinner," eating only foods that are different shades of green.

- Learn a new sport that stresses right-brain thinking. (tennis, skiing, golf, skating, or gymnastics)

44

started but not finished. Becky is a doer but not always a finisher. Her favorite comment after getting into an activity is, "Boring!" It takes a lot of energy as well as patience to keep up with Becky's enthusiasm and varied, changing interests.

ACCEPTING BECKY'S LEADING RIGHT BRAIN

There was a time when her parents thought Becky might have a hearing problem. She just didn't seem to pay attention like her siblings. They soon learned to accept her short attention span and realized that Becky is a dreamer. Many times her parents see that faraway look in her eyes and know that she is "gone," creating a myriad of images in her mind.

Becky is a doer. She grows impatient with written directions. Quite often she visualizes the whole problem then combines the images she has created with her intuitive abilities to come up with a solution. She will do what "feels right inside" without really being able to explain logically her reasoning. When she does get things done, it's not always in a logical, sequential manner—a behavior particularly frustrating to Becky's left-brained father!

In an effort to support Becky's rather disorganized nature, she has been given her own "piggy place" at home. Her parents realize her need to put things in piles instead of files! (Not in the whole house, mind you, just in her bedroom!) Her room is filled with projects,

If Becky had her way, the whole world would be surrounded by giant stereo speakers. She loves music as a background for learning. She loves to do three or four things at once, and she says the music "ties it all together" for her. Her parents are amazed at how Becky can talk on the phone to music, eat to music, sleep to music, and do her homework to music. What seems to be a distraction to other family members appears to be a help, if not a necessity, for Becky.

STRETCHING BECKY'S LEFT BRAIN

Once we have accepted Becky, the right-brain thinker, the next step is to encourage the development of Becky, the whole-brain thinker. When the two hemispheres cooperate, they produce an understanding and learning synergy that equals much more than the sum of the two parts. From the time Becky was four years old, her mother has used color, bright-changing patterns, and simple animal shapes to help her daughter be more organized. Color coding the dresser

45

drawers with Contact paper (socks in the blue drawer, play clothes in the yellow drawer) has helped to get Becky's clothes off the floor and into some semblance of order.

The family calendar is large enough to glue pictures and printed messages on it. The whole family knows that the best way to remind Becky of an important date is not just to tell her about it but show her about it. If there is a picture of Grandma glued to the 25th, Becky will quickly ask why it is there. The image in her brain created by the photograph will help her remember to send that all-important birthday card.

In an effort to stretch his daughter's logical and sequential thinking abilities, Becky's father is slowly, but persistently teaching her to play cards, checkers, and chess. These are games that stimulate both left- and right-hemisphere thinking. In Becky's case, they will help her look at parts or individual

choices in a game. She needs to see the trees, not just the forest.

To improve her listening skills and lengthen her attention span, Becky is encouraged to doodle while she listens. Even manipulating a small piece of clay helps a right-brained thinker process spoken information and directions better.

Finally, whenever possible, the family tries to arrive a little early to meetings, family gatherings, plays, and sporting events. This will allow Becky some extra time to center her attention and focus her brain on the situation at hand.

Becky is a "fiddler." It takes her longer to get ready to do things. The technical term for such behavior is "delayed closure." Right-brained people who delay closure are guided by an unconscious feeling of what they are to do. Presumably, they formulate the problem below the threshold of awareness before beginning to solve the problem. Becky is a good problem solver, but many times in school, her classmates are half finished before she has begun. Her report card reflects her "fiddling." Many times very creative, "spacy," right-brained children will not be good "grade-getters" in school. Fortunately for Becky, her parents realize that her particular school advocates a very left-brained environment. All the more reason why they try to expose her to more right-brained activities at home.

Now you know the rest of the story! Keep reading and keep talking to other parents of gifted children. Communication is the key! Parenting gifted children may well be the greatest challenge of a parent's life. Teaching gifted children may well be the greatest challenge of an educator's career. We are all in this together!

BIRTH ORDER

Does It Make a Difference?

Robin, Joey, Cindy, and Lynn have been buddies all the way through school. They are all in the sixth grade, and they are all gifted. When you pull their cumulative folders from the school files, several similarities come to the surface: large vocabulary, intense curiosity, high-level thinker, good memory, adult sense of humor, good worker, and intense worry. However, there is one seemingly unimportant piece of data that might go undetected by even the most interested parent or educator. Three of them, Joey, Robin, and Lynn, are firstborn children. Cindy is the "baby" of her family. Does birth order have anything to do with giftedness? Some educators believe firstborn children have a better chance to be gifted because of the way they are nurtured by their parents. The listings in *Who's Who in American Colleges and Universities* indicate that a majority of the members are the oldest children from two-child and three-child families. Freud theorized that one's numerical position in the family (firstborn, secondborn, "baby") was a strong clue in his/her personality development. Although there is no research that definitively states how birth order affects giftedness, success in life, and personality, perhaps the following information will help parents improve their nurturing skills.

CHARACTERISTICS OF THE FIRSTBORN

- Self-confident, autocratic, independent
- Sensitive, conscientious, studious
- Ambitious, individualistic, perfectionist
- Persistent, leader, outspoken
- Good listener, shy (in early years)
- More confidence in making decisions
- High achiever (good grades in school)

Of course, parents play an important role in the development of these characteristics. Parents seem to do more with their firstborn child. More interaction and more attention is paid to the child. Mom and Dad actually talk more to him/her. As a result, a very strong bond or attachment is established early between parent and child. In addition to the above characteristics, the firstborn child is breast-fed longer, rewarded more often, and overprotected. After all, he/she is the center of attention most of the time so he/she quickly learns to expect praise. One final interesting point: firstborn are usually planned children.

If that all sounds like the good news, you're right! Now for a little bad news. Parents quite often set standards that are much too high for their firstborn children. They want the best for them; they try to give the best to them, but they also expect the very best from them. Many firstborn children are afraid to fail because they are pushed so hard to succeed. They plan ahead. They worry about the future. Studies show that firstborn children are punished more and spanked more severely than their siblings. Psychologists find these children more likely to be riddled with anxiety and worry. They have great difficulty *accepting* help from others because they are usually expected to *give* help to their siblings and parents. Most of this bad news can be chalked up to inexperience in childrearing.

There is another kind of firstborn child that also has some interesting characteristics to add to the birth-order theories—the only child. Since an only child is also firstborn, he/she possesses many of the same characteristics. In fact, much of the research lumps the two together. However, there are additional points worth mentioning. An only child does not have to compete with siblings so is even more self-assured and confident than firstborn children.

They are very independent but may not be as outgoing in the early years. As adults, many times they are characterized as private people. Age-peer friendships are very important to them. They choose their friends carefully and rely on only one or two really close friends. However, they feel comfortable with most adults since they had more contact with them at an early age.

Parents usually have more money to spend on an only child. More experiences, more toys, and more learning materials and equipment do make a difference. These children tend to be assertive, aggressive, and strong leaders. They like to be the boss! However, they tend to hide their true feelings and benefit from the help given by an older authority figure.

CHARACTERISTICS OF THE MIDDLE CHILD

- Self-pitying, dissatisfied, fun-loving
- Unconventional, laid-back, placid
- Unpredictable, easygoing, social
- Moody, less academic, maverick
- Competitive, class clown

The middle child has the roughest time in many families. Being in the middle is similar to being in "no man's land." The middle child has difficulty knowing who he/she is. It is difficult for him/her to exhibit a true personality. Many times he/she is denied the privileges of the firstborn as well as the freedoms of the youngest member of the family. Being caught in the middle, he/she must do many things that may not fit his/her personality just to get some attention! (That's why the above list of characteristics may seem ambiguous.)

Middle children develop a "Hey, remember me?" behavior pattern. Much of their motivation comes from resentment. What follows is an "I give up" attitude, which leads to a devil-may-care or happy-go-lucky personality. They don't worry as much as firstborn children. When a stressful situation arises, they move into a *Pitiful Pearl* personality so they don't have to take responsibility. Middle children can quite easily be social butterflies; they love being around people and seemed starved for attention. However, they appear to be more vulnerable to peer pressures and become victims quite easily. They are definitely followers, not leaders. Expect middle children to be late bloomers. It takes them awhile to find their place in the world.

CHARACTERISTICS OF THE YOUNGEST CHILD

- Clever, ingenious, demanding
- Charming, innovative, creative
- Ambitious, mercurial, lazy
- Imaginative, self-centered, restless
- Egotistical, spontaneous, nonconformist

Well, parents, are you ready? This is the spoiled child. The "baby" of the family usually has it the easiest in many families. There is no doubt about it—this child is special. He/She gets the most attention. Of course, Grandpa and Grandma must share in giving this flood of attention. After all, he/she is their last grandchild, second only in importance to their first grandchild! The "baby" of the family has the most freedom. It allows the child's real personality to emerge. Parents are not as demanding or pushy. They pamper this child more, punish less, and expect less.

The youngest child in a family is given the least amount of responsibility. However, because the youngest does not learn the meaning of responsibility as a child, he/she has great difficulty accepting responsibility when an adult. In some cases, he/she has been waited on hand and foot as a youngster and expects that to continue through adulthood. As a result, the youngest may have difficulty adjusting to a true partnership in marriage.

Life has its bumpy places for the "baby" of the family, too. He/She is teased more by brothers and sisters, and since parents rely more on the older siblings to take care of the youngest, the "baby" grows up with a rather mixed impression of who's boss.

The youngest in the family does want to be taken seriously. The child wants to find his/her own special place in the world, too, even if he/she bends the rules once in awhile to get there!

CONCLUSION

Wouldn't it be nice, parents, if you could combine all the "right stuff" in raising each child in your family and thereby become a perfect parent? But there are no absolutes in life or in research. There are exceptions to all rules. Just because many gifted children are firstborn doesn't mean all gifted children are firstborn. And just because a child happens to be in the middle doesn't mean he/she isn't gifted. The analogy goes on and on. Take Brad Anderson, for example. He has an I.Q. of 149. But he doesn't have brothers, sisters, or parents. He's an orphan waiting to be adopted. No, there really are no absolutes, There is a book, though, entitled *Leo the Late Bloomer* by Robert Kraus. It's for all parents who love their kids, try as hard as they can to be good parents, but still get frustrated and fail once in awhile.

"BUT I DON'T WANT TO BE GIFTED!"

There it is—a file folder full of potential: high IQ scores, graphs and charts with marks to indicate the ninety-ninth percentile, I.E.P.'s (Individual Education Plans), computer readouts, teacher checklists, parent checklists, and even student checklists. It's all there, all the "right" data—proof positive that this child is gifted. So what's the problem?

As we dig deeper into this maze of numbers, points, and scores, the inconsistencies begin to surface. There are report cards with roller coaster grades, everything from straight As to Ds. There are handwritten notes from frustrated teachers and parents: "This child is bright, but he has such poor handwriting." "She isn't working up to her potential, doesn't seem to be motivated." "He deliberately failed a history test, even though he knew all the

answers." "She really seems to enjoy math but is so slow at getting her other work finished." "He is such a perfectionist." "She has a poor attitude about herself and school." "He asked to be removed from the gifted program. No reason given." And so it goes. This folder full of potential reads like a war diary, a chronicle of battles, some won, some lost. We find one problem after another, one recommendation after another, all in the name of education.

IS IT ANY WONDER...?

The word is *gifted*—a six-letter word that makes some gifted children cringe. Why? First, it is definitely a learned attitude, most often from adults. Parents who hesitate to admit in public that their child is gifted are sending a message to their child that giftedness may be something of which to be ashamed. School

50

administrators do the same thing when they attach vague, cute titles to gifted programs. (Call the program anything, but just don't use the word gifted!) Instead of pride and confidence in establishing a program that meets the needs of certain students who happen to be gifted, there is fear and resentment—fear that such a program will "stir up" community resentment toward gifted students because they don't deserve a special program. Some classroom teachers reinforce the "gifted is a bad word" philosophy when they constantly remind gifted children of their weaknesses. They condition gifted children into being average or into thinking they are average. Parents and educators have a tendency to withhold praise from gifted children because they **expect** them to do superior work. They have the mistaken idea that gifted children don't need as much praise and reinforcement as other children. Is it any wonder that gifted children quickly develop a resentment toward giftedness?

"It wouldn't be so bad if I didn't have to be gifted all the time." (Bryan, Age 5)

"Giftedness is not something you earn. " (Dr. Walter Barbe)

"It ain't easy being green. " (Kermit the Frog)

Bryan, Walter, and Kermit are extraordinary philosophers. They know. They understand what it means to be different. The pressure placed on gifted children by parents, teachers, and society in general must seem unbearable at times. Dr. Judy Roseberry, Unified School District, Garden Grove, California, also understands. She has responded to the pressures with the following:

Premises of the Demands of Giftedness:

- High level intelligence makes certain demands upon the gifted child.
- Behavior of gifted children results from these demands.
- There are curriculum implications inherent in these demands.

A gifted child's behavior often reflects the following demands:

- To crave for knowledge, to satisfy the need to feel progress in what he/she is learning.
- To feel the need to focus on or devour a subject.
- To make observations, to see relationships.
- To place high standards on himself/herself.
- To be creative or inventive, to seek an unusual or unique approach to an assignment.
- To question generalizations.
- To be serious-minded, to be intolerant (usually) of foolishness or silliness.

51

- To concentrate, to become totally absorbed in a task, to have a longer attention span.

- To explore wide interests at a maturity beyond his/her chronological age.

- To be sensitive to honor and truth.

- To express ideas and reactions (sometimes being seen as argumentative).

- To resist routine, drill; to require unique ways of pursuing drill.

- To work alone.

- To be intolerant of stupidity.

- To seek order, structure, consistency.

- To do critical, evaluative thinking (possibly leading to a critical attitude toward self and others).

- To be rarely satisfied with the simple and obvious.

- To be impatient with sloppy or disorganized thinking.

- To have his/her intelligence responded to.

- To seek out his/her mental peers.

- To be friendly and outgoing.

- To use his/her power of abstraction, to see and point out cause and effect relationships.

- To have time for thinking, solitude.

- To pursue a learning pace of his/her own.

- To be outstanding in many areas but average in others.

As difficult as these demands may be for parents and educators to respond to, just imagine what it would be like to live with them every single day. Is it any wonder. . . ?

- **Problem:** In many schools gifted students must leave the regular classroom in order to participate in a gifted program. In some of these pull-out programs, the gifted students are forced to do twice as much paperwork because they are required to make up the work they miss in the regular classroom as well as complete the work in the gifted program. In effect, they are being punished for being gifted.

   Solution: Gifted students should be held responsible for the **learning** they are missing in the regular classroom **but not necessarily for the work.** Classroom teachers can administer pretests or posttests that can easily determine whether a gifted child has already mastered a skill.

- **Problem:** Some parents use their gifted children as social status symbols. They impose unrealistic goals and expectations on their children, which can result in feelings of inadequacy accompanied by fear of failure.

Solution: Membership in an organization for parents of gifted students can be very helpful in raising the awareness level of parents who may be putting too much pressure on their gifted children. The interaction with other parents of gifted children is very effective. In addition, school counselors, gifted program coordinators, and/or psychologists should also be involved in solving this problem—the sooner, the better!

- **Problem:** A gifted child may withdraw into a private shell if he/she is not being challenged. Since the gifted are capable of divergent thinking, they may feel their own responses are wrong because they fall outside the realm of what is generally accepted. They need to see themselves as part of a whole society.

Solution: Finding a mentor for a gifted child offers a unique form of individualized instruction and self-directed learning. A mentor can help a student explore his strengths and weaknesses while improving his understanding of the relationship between school and the outside world. "Mentoring is the gifted tutoring the gifted, and underlines the importance of their being one of their own, as well as society's, best resources for realizing learning potentials." (Runions, 1980)

- **Problem:** Sometimes gifted children suffer verbal abuse from children who are not gifted. As a result, many gifted

children will go through phases of trying to hide their true abilities.

Solution: Children's literature contains some examples of the gifted child and that child's relationship with others. For children who are classmates of a gifted child, literature can help their understanding, too, of what it is like to be different.

The following book list suggests recommended reading for educators and parents of gifted children. Portions of the list are taken from Eileen Tway's "The Gifted Child in Literature," The National Council of Teachers of English, January, 1980.

The Gifted Child as Different and Learning to Cope:

Exploring the Lives of Gifted People: The Arts, Kathy Balsamo (Good Apple, 1987)

Exploring the Lives of Gifted People: The Sciences, Kathy Balsamo (Good Apple, 1987)

Henry III, Joseph Krumgold (Atheneum, 1967)

A Wrinkle in Time, Madeleine L'Engle (Farrar, Straus & Giroux, 1962)

A Wind in the Door, Madeleine L'Engle (Farrar, Straus & Giroux, 1973)

A Swiftly Tilting Planet, Madeleine L'Engle (Farrar, Straus & Giroux, 1973)

The Rare One, Pamela Rogers (Thomas Nelson, 1973)

The Girl Called Al, Constancy Green (Viking, 1969)

A Tide Flowing, Eleanor Spence (Oxford Press, 1976)

I Am Not a Short Adult, Marilyn Burns (Little, Brown, & Co., 1977)

Jonathan Livingston Seagull, Richard Bach (Avon, 1970)

The Gifted Child in School:

Hugo and Josephine, Maria Gripe (Dell, 1969)

Freaky Friday, Mary Rodgers (Harper & Row, 1972)

A Wind in the Door, Madeleine L'Engle (Farrar, Straus & Giroux, 1973)

What Makes You So Special, Sherri Heller (Thinking CAPS, 1975)

Leo the Late Bloomer, Robert Kraus (Windmill Books, 1971)

Special Traumas of the Gifted Child

Don't Burn Down the Birthday Cake, Joe Wayman (Heartstone Press, 1988)

If You Promise Not To Tell (Record Album/Activity Book), Joe Wayman (Good Apple, Inc., 1985)

The Hall of Fame, Franny McAleer (Mafex, 1983)

Where the Sidewalk Ends, Shel Silverstein (Harper & Row, 1974)

How To Eat like a Child and Other lessons in Not Being a Grown-Up, Delia Ephron (Viking, 1978)

Father's Arcane Daughter, E.L. Konigsburg (Atheneum, 1976)

The Great Gilly Hopkins, Katherine Paterson (Thomas Crowell, 1978)

George, E.L. Konigsburg (Atheneum, 1972)

Reaching Out to Others

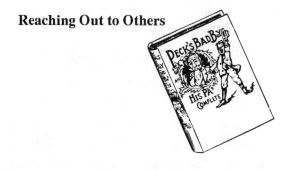

Jennifer, Hecate, Macbeth, William McKinley, and Me, Elizabeth, E.L. Konigsburg (Atheneum, 1968)

Beyond Another Door, Sonia Levitin (Atheneum, 1977)

Don't Play Dead Before You Have To, Maria Wojciechowska (Harper & Row, 1970)

Being True to Oneself:

Words by Heart, Quida Sebestzen (Little, Brown, & Co., 1979)

A Sound of Chariots, Mollie Hunter (Harper & Row, 1972)

One is One, Barbara Leonie Picard (Hold, 1966)

Special Gifts:

Pennington's Last Term, K.M. Peyton (Thomas Crowell, 1971)

The Beethoven Medal, K.M. Peyton (Thomas Crowell, 1972)

A Gift of Magic, Lois Duncan (Little, Brown, & Co., 1971)

Absolute Zero, Helen Cresswell (Macmillan, 1978).

And This is Laura, Ellen Conford (Little, Brown, & Co., 1977)

The Bat Poet, Randall Jarrell (Macmillan, 1963)

Pennington's Heir, K,M. Peyton (Crowell, 1973)

There are more problems, of course, and more solutions—some known, some yet to be discovered. The war goes on, battle by battle. It makes one wonder, though, why anybody would really **want** to be gifted. When we **need** gifted people so much, why do we make it so difficult for them? Are we losing the war? No. Attitudes are changing, gifted programs are surviving, and funding is improving. We still lose a battle now and then. Some gifted students are still dropping out of high school. And of those who don't, 50 percent are still considered underachievers; so the fight goes on. Victory isn't just around the corner, but it's there—in the dream of parents of gifted children. In the meantime, we keep file folders (war diaries) of the "right" data.

RESOURCES

Galbraith, Judy. *The Gifted Kids Survival Guide Ages 10 & Under.* Minneapolis: Free Spirit Publishing Company, 1984.

Goertzel, Victor and Mildred. *Cradles of Eminence.* Boston: Little, Brown, & Company, 1962.

Houston, Jean. *The Possible Human.* Boston: J.P. Tarcher, Inc., 1982.

Runions, Ted. "The Mentor Academy Program: Educating the Gifted and Talented for the 80's." *Gifted Child Quarterly.* Fall, 1980.

Webb, James T., Elizabeth Mechstroth, and Stephanie Tolan. *Guiding the Gifted Child.* Columbus, OH: Ohio Psychology Publishing Company, 1982.

DISCOVERING THE MAGIC: YOUR CHILD'S CREATIVITY

It was a very special gift. After all, it's not every day that a friend buys you a puppet. Steiff Puppets are especially wonderful because they look so real. This one was a beautiful gray rabbit – all soft and cuddly – just waiting for the right hands to bring it to life. I asked the daughter of one of my workshop participants to help me think of a proper name. I was prepared for her to choose a name like Fuzzy or Flopsy. To my surprise, she didn't answer immediately but instead asked for a little time to think about it. After two days of careful deliberation, she announced with much confidence her choice of names. "Well," she said, "my best friend's name is Sherry and my Grandpa's name is Herbert, so I think you should call the rabbit 'Sherbert'!"

Sherbert has traveled thousands of miles with me to hundreds of workshops. (I finally had to retire him last year – terminal jet lag!) But I miss him. Most of all I miss sharing the experience of how he got his name. It must be magic, that sparkle that shines in children's eyes when knowledge, experience, joy, and courage combine with language to form new ideas. Most of the time adults miss it, or just take it for granted. There is a name for that sparkle, that **magic.** Educators call it **creativity.** They have spent years using cold hard facts and figures to try and explain what is probably unexplainable. They try to teach children to be creative. It's no wonder we have so much trouble. You can't teach children to be creative because they already are! But adults (especially American adults) are constantly trying to fix things that don't need to be fixed. We must stop trying to make children creative and just ALLOW IT TO HAPPEN!

How do we know it's already there? Just watch your child and listen. Children will "give themselves away" with the things they say and the things they do. Perhaps a look at some facts based on research will get you off to a good start in your search for the magic.

WHAT TO LOOK FOR

Studies at the Institute for Personality, Assessment and Research (IPAR) include three categories of creative people: the artistically creative, the scientifically creative, and those with the combined qualities of both artist and scientist. Those persons studied were writers, painters, architects, mathematicians, research workers in engineering and science, and independent inventors. The following is from "Development of Creativity." Creative persons were characterized as:

- Being original, curious, cognitively flexible.
- Using their intelligence effectively.
- Being not generally well rounded and having many one-sided interests. Preferring complexity, tolerating clutter and ambiguity, and resisting premature closure.
- Being open to experience, searching for beauty, and having strong theoretical and aesthetic interests.
- Prefering the "whole" rather than small details.
- Taking risks, reaching farther for original solutions, and combining elements.
- Integrating reason and passion, reconciling the rational and irrational, and perceiving intuitively.
- Experiencing inner awareness of the outer world.
- Accepting in themselves opposite-sex characteristics.
- Exhibiting a "sense of destiny" and a strong ego identity.
- Creative behavior beings at birth and increases year by year. If this behavior is suppressed or ridiculed, the joy of creative thinking and activity is likely to be replaced by apathy, shame, or guilt. To allow creativity to happen, we must communicate a positive attitude about the characteristics described above.

TWENTY-THREE SIGNALS OF CREATIVITY: A CHECKLIST FOR PARENTS

Creativity is a key component in most definitions of giftedness. Following are twenty-three characteristics that signal creativity in children and some sample statements by children that reflect those traits. This list was developed by E. Paul Torrance, distinguished professor of educational psychology at the University of Georgia. While few children will display all of the characteristics, the presence of several of them in combination indicate a creative promise in your child that should be nurtured at home and school.

- Intense absorption in listening, observing, or doing: "But I didn't hear you call me for dinner."

- Intense animation and physical involvement: "But I can't sit still—I'm thinking."

- Use of analogies in speech: "I feel like a caterpillar waiting to become a butterfly."

- Tendency to challenge ideas of authority: "Why do I have to go to school until I am sixteen?"

- Habit of checking many sources: "Mom, I looked at all the books and watched a TV special and asked my teacher, and I still cannot figure out where God lives."

- Taking a close look at things: "Hey, this centipede only has ninety-nine legs!"

- Eagerness to tell others about discoveries: "Guess what!" Guess what! Guess what!"

- Continuing in creative activities after scheduled quitting time: "I did my art work right through recess!"

- Showing relationships among apparently unrelated ideas: "Hey, Mom, your new hat looks just like a flying saucer!"

- Following an idea through: "Tomorrow I'm going to dig for gold in our backyard."

- Various manifestations of curiosity and wanting to know: "I just wanted to know what the yard looked like from the top of the roof."

- Spontaneous use of discovery or experimental approval: "I thought flour and water would make bread, but all I got was white goo."

- Excitement in the voice about discoveries: "Flour and water make paste!"

- Habit of guessing and testing outcomes: "I put detergent in the bird bath, but no birds came to clean up. May I try some bubble bath today?"

- Honesty and intense search for the truth: "Mom, I hope this won't upset you, but I don't think there is a tooth fairy."

- Independent action: "There are no good books on racing cars, Dad. I am going to write my own."

- Boldness of new ideas: "But I think that children should be allowed to vote."

- Difficult to distract: "I cannot come out to play. I'm waiting for my chemicals to dissolve."

- Manipulations of ideas and objects to obtain new combinations: "I'm going to take this string and this pencil and make a compass."

- Penetrating observations and questions: "When the snow melts, where does the white go?"

- Tendency to seek alternatives and explore new possibilities: "This old shoe would make a great flowerpot."

- Self-initiated learning: "Yesterday I went to the library and checked out all the books on dinosaurs."

- Willingness to consider or toy with new ideas: "What if dogs were masters and people were pets?"

Blocks to Creativity. J. Zinker refers to a series of "blocks to creativity" which summarize many of the problems in the development of creativity. The blocks to creativity include:

- **Rigidity** in stereotyped reactions, over-emphasis on traditions and necessary conformity.

- **Fear** of failure and of the unknown.

- **Avoidance** of frustration.

- **Reluctance** to play, to exert influence, to let go.

- **Difficulty** with ambiguity and complexity.

- **Sensory dullness,** or impoverished fantasy life, holding back emotions or spontaneity.

- **Lacking** "wholeness" polarization.

- **Low self-evaluation,** or failure to see own strengths.

Many of the above blocks to creativity can be overcome by simply allowing and encouraging your child to play. Play allows children to explore new ideas in a safe way, to freely express emotions, to struggle in solving problems in different ways, and to work things out for themselves. Parents should encourage children to play with imaginary friends and act out make-believe situations. Such drama will permit a child to express both positive and negative emotions. Sandra W. Russ, associate professor of psychology at Case Western University, says play releases "forbidden emotion," such as aggression. Play makes dangerous thoughts not so dangerous.

She recommends that the best thing a parent can do to increase fantasy play is simply to encourage it. When you see fantasy play, stay out of it and don't engage in it. Create a permissive atmosphere. Probably the best piece of advice Ms. Russ has to offer comes in the form of a warning. She cautions parents not to involve their child in too many activities. Children need time for themselves, and telling a child not to play fantasy games or involving him/her in too many organized activities can stifle creative growth.

Another approach to allowing creativity to happen is to chip away at the "mental locks" that close minds. Roger von Oech is the author of a delightful book entitled *A Whack on the Side of the Head*. In it he describes the ten most common inhibitions ("locks") to creativity. Some of the worst include: follow the rules, be practical, and always find a right answer. He offers several tips for opening these locks. If none of the approaches work, he administers a metaphorical "whack on the side of the head" to dislodge the blocks to creative impulses. If a child becomes overly practical, for instance, he advises that the parent or teacher ask "what if" questions that force the child to use his/her imagination. Von Oech also practices what he preaches. He proudly displays a doctorate in the history of ideas that he received from Stanford University in 1975—a degree that he proposed to the university and of which he is the sole recipient!

CONCLUSION

I wish I could have been there to see the sparkle in Sister Tabatha Babbett's eyes the day she watched two men laboriously sawing wood with a straight-blade saw and at the same time looked down at her spinning wheel. The Shaker woman figured that the men's job would be much easier if sawteeth were cut into the edge of the wheel. The result: a circular saw blade was invented.

Magic!

I wish I could have been there when Eli Whitney conjured up the cotton gin by watching a cat trying to catch a chicken through a fence - just the thing to comb seeds out of cotton bolls!

Magic!

I wish I could have been there when the NASA designers were trying to find a fastening device for space suits that astronauts could manipulate with their bulky gloves. During a word-association exercise/fantasy someone came up with the words "rain forest." One of the team members imagined himself running through a forest and having thorns stick in his clothes. That gave the group the idea of making a fastener that gripped with thousands of thornlike fibers. The result: Velcro.

Magic!

I wish I could be with you as you discover the magic in your children. Let me make one last attempt to explain the unexplainable. To quote what Nobel Prize-winning physician Albert Szent-Gyorgyi, "Discovery consists of seeing what everybody else has seen and thinking what nobody else has thought."

RESOURCES

Alvino, James, and the Editors of Gifted Child Monthly. *Parents' Guide to Raising a Gifted Child*. Boston: Little, Brown & Company, 1985.

Bruch, Catherine B., Professor in the Department of Educational Psychology. "Development of Creativity." University of Georgia, Athens: GA.

Madigan, Carol Orsay and Ann Elwood. *Brainstorms and Thunderbolts*. New York: Macmillan Publishing Company, 1984.

Von Oech, Roger. *A Whack on the Side of the Head*. New York: Warner Books, Inc., 1983.

DISCIPLINE — WITH A DIFFERENCE

Gifted children are like plants that need stakes to grow against, with gentle ties where necessary to support their natural growth, instead of being rigidly espaliered to a stone wall in artificial designs someone else devised. (Stephanie Tolan)

What do you consider your most helpful and valuable resource in raising your gifted child? During one parent session, without hesitation, a young woman stood up and proclaimed in a loud voice, "The Bathroom!" After some gentle inquiry on my part, we learned of her frustration at trying to discipline her five-year-old gifted son. She went on to explain, "My neighbor to the south says her kids drive her to drink! My neighbor across the street says her kids drive her to her knees in prayer! Well, mine drive me to the peace and quiet and solitude of my bathroom!"

Across the meeting room I saw smiles and nods of agreement. Thank goodness, indeed, for small rooms with locks on the doors. Parents of a gifted child have the responsibility to develop their child's abilities in all areas: intellectual, aesthetic, physical, emotional, social, and moral. What a job! It's too bad children aren't like pancakes. You always throw away the first ones you make, trying again and again until you get some good ones. No, our gifted children are much too precious to "throw away." We must try our best to help them "turn out right" the first time. Discipline is an important part of that development.

To begin with, gifted children are different. Yes, we are constantly reminded that they are children first and gifted second—children, rather than small adults, with social and emotional needs that usually match closely with their chronological age rather than their mental age. However, some of the more traditional methods of disciplining children, such as punishment, are not always as effective with gifted children. Dr. James Webb (*Guiding the Gifted Child*) believes it is vital to distinguish between discipline and punishment: "Punishment is largely a negative term—a negative concept. Discipline, on the other hand, can be positive. Discipline means teaching a child self-control so that he/she will ultimately be able to incorporate values and standards into his/her life in order to interact responsibly with others in predictable, mutually satisfying ways. Discipline can be a loving pattern that helps your child learn alternatives. It is an opportunity for your child to discover and depend upon his/her own power."

GROWING PAINS

Perhaps if we examine some of the characteristics of gifted children and problems associated with these characteristics, we can gain a better understanding of what it means to be gifted. And with that understanding perhaps we will gain a better insight into how to discipline our gifted children.

Characteristics*	Problems
Keen power of observation; naive receptivity, sense of the significant; willingness to examine the unusual	Possible gullibility; social rejection
Power of abstraction, conceptualization, synthesis; interest in inductive learning and problem solving; pleasure in intellectual activity	Occasional resistance to direction, rejection or omission of detail
Interest in cause-effect relations, ability to see relationships; interest in applying concepts; love of truth	Difficulty in accepting the illogical
Desire for structure and order; desire for consistency, as in value systems, number systems, clocks, calendars	Invention of own systems, sometimes conflicting
Retentiveness	Dislike for routine and drill; need for early mastery of foundation skills
Questioning attitude, intellectual curiosity, inquisitive mind; intrinsic motivation	"Smart Brain — Smart Mouth"
Power of critical thinking; skepticism, evaluative testing; self-criticism and self-checking	Critical attitude toward others, discouragement from self-criticism
Creativeness and inventiveness; liking for new ways of doing things; interest in creating, brainstorming, free-wheeling	Rejection of the known; need to invent for oneself
Power of concentration; intense attention that excludes all else; long attention span	Resistance to interruption
Persistent, goal-directed behavior	Stubbornness
Sensitivity, intuitiveness; empathy for others; need for emotional support and sympathetic attitude; ego-involvement; need for courage	Need for success and recognition; sensitivity to criticism; vulnerability to peer group rejection
High enery, alertness, eagerness; periods of intense voluntary effort preceding invention	Parent and peer group pressures and nonconformity; problems of rejection and rebellion
Independence in work and study; preference for individualized work; self-reliance; need for freedom of movement and action; need to live; loneliness	Lack of homogeneity in group work; need for flexibility and individualization; need for help in exploring and developing interests; need to build basic competencies in major interests
Versatility and virtuosity; diversity of interests and abilities; interest in many hobbies; proficiency in art forms such as music and drawing	Need for peer group relations in many types of groups; problems in developing social leadership
Friendliness and outgoingness	Frustration with inactivity and absence of progress

(*Adapted from *Mansokie*, Central Oklahoma Mensa, Oct. 1980 — Stan Fuller, Editor)

Suppose we focus on one characteristic (questioning attitude, intellectual curiosity, inquisitive mind; intrinsic motivation) and its concomitant problem ("Smart Brain-Smart Mouth"). I have yet to meet a gifted child who didn't have countless questions bottled up inside. Parents must allow gifted children to ask questions. The gifted child must be made to feel comfortable with the idea of asking questions. However, always knowing the right answer to the child's questions is not as important as one might think. What is important is honesty. Your gifted child will learn to respect a sincere "I don't know the answer to that question." Searching for the answer TOGETHER can be a challenging and rewarding experience.

HOW a gifted child asks questions can either interest and stimulate adults or frustrate and anger them. Parents can teach their gifted children better ways of phrasing questions or making suggestions. Adults, especially teachers, are much more receptive to "In my opinion. . ." rather than "That's stupid. I have a better idea." Dr. Judy Roseberry suggests that what the gifted need is training and practice in using the following "Survival Phrases":

"In my opinion . . ."

"I respectfully disagree with that statement because . . ."

"It seems as if . . ."

"Have you thought about this possibility as it relates to . . ."

"May I express my opinion concerning . . ."

"Could it be that you have overlooked this point because . . ."

By practicing and practicing and practicing these phrases at home, parents are giving their gifted child survival skills for succeeding in an adult world.

Parents should use the phrases too. The philosophy "Do as I say—not as I do" just doesn't hold water with gifted kids!

PARENTS WHO MAKE A DIFFERENCE

. . . are models. "People seldom improve when they have no other model but themselves to copy after." (Oliver Goldsmith)

. . . encourage their gifted child to assume responsibility for his/her own behavior. One of the most effective ways to do this is to allow the child to experience the natural consequences of his/her behavior. For example, if your gifted child has decided that he/she will not do homework, the natural consequence for that behavior will probably be a low or failing grade. Trying to force the child to do

the homework with punishment, threats, or bribes only deprives the child of experiencing the natural consequences of the decision not to do the homework.

. . . do not point out unacceptable behavior to their gifted child at the same time they remind him/her that he/she is gifted. Ex-

ample: "You're so smart—you're supposed to be gifted. You should know better!" Relating unacceptable behavior to giftedness only stimulates negative feelings about giftedness and creates a poor self-concept.

. . . are honest. They respond in an open, frank manner to ALL their gifted child's questions. They do not make fun of or gossip about their child's abilities. Playing games with a child's mind and self-respect only results in disrespect and mistrust.

. . . do not "exhibit" their gifted child as a social status symbol. There is a difference between pushing and stretching your child. When the expectations are too high and the spirit of competitiveness too intense, the ten-

sions created hamper rather than encourage self-discipline.

. . . avoid overscheduling their gifted child's life. Children need time to think, to be alone, to dream, and to make their own choices. Gifted children cannot be expected to be high achievers and top performers all the time.

. . . allow their gifted child to fail, to misbehave, and to be human. Being gifted may mean you have a gifted mind, but it doesn't always mean you have a gifted mouth or a gifted body or gifted behavior!

. . . set limits. Rules are important—they give a sense of security and stability. Just don't overdo it. You may need to set fewer rules for gifted children, but when the rules are broken, BE CONSISTENT in following through with the consequences. Gifted children are masters at testing your consistency!

. . . accentuate the positive. Praise is a powerful force in motivating desirable behavior. Unfortunately, some gifted children get attention from their parents only when they are being disciplined. Some parents have difficulty giving praise to their children because they were not raised with praise themselves. Giving compliments takes practice!

NOTE: Putting compliments and encouragement in writing is particularly effective. A quick note found at just the right time will reinforce desirable behavior.

. . . never stop trying to COMMUNICATE. Dialogue involves LISTENING to the child, responding on a one-to-one level with honest respect, and treating the child as a unique individual. Parents should reject only the undesirable behavior, not the child. They should discuss with the child all the possible choices, evaluate the consequences, and encourage the sharing of personal feelings. Example: "How do you think you would feel if you did that? How do you think other people would feel? What do you think would probably happen if you did that? Tell me all the possibilities." Remember the formula: COMMUNICATION = FEELINGS AND CHOICES.

THE RIGHT STUFF

The message conveyed in the movie *The Right Stuff* can easily be applied to the parenting of gifted children. Moreover, in their book *Cradles of Eminence,* Victor and Mildred Goertzel discuss the characteristics of parents of four hundred gifted men and women of the twentieth century. They discovered a strong drive toward intellectual and creative achievement in one or both of the parents. The parents of these celebrities were curious, experimental, restless, and seeking. They were physically driving, high energy, intellectually striving people. They respected learning and loved truth and beauty. They touched their gifted children—both physically and emotionally. They loved their children by setting rules for them and by setting examples as risk takers. In short, they had "the right stuff."

Remember, parents, hold on to your sense of humor! When all else fails, take a step back, take a deep breath, take one day at a time, and take comfort in the knowledge that there were and are thousands of parents of gifted children thinking and feeling the same things. What do you suppose Mrs. Edison did when little Tommy, while trying to emulate birds, sat on eggs and ended up smashing them—all over a new couch! And what do you suppose Mr. Einstein had to say to his neighbors when Albert made up his own religion and went about chanting hymns he'd composed?

RESOURCES

Colangelo, Nicholas, and Ronald T. Zaffrann. *New Voices in Counseling the Gifted.* Dubuque, IA: Kendall/Hunt Publishing Company, 1979.

Dreikurs, R. *The Challenge of Parenthood.* New York: Duell, Sloan & Pearce, 1958.

Ginott, H.G. *Between Parent and Child.* New York: Avon, 1965.

Goertzel, Victor and Mildred. *Cradles of Eminence.* Boston: Little, Brown & Company, 1962.

Ward, Sharon. "Tips for the Parents of Gifted Students." *Missouri Schools.* March, 1980. p.1.

Webb, James T., Elizabeth Mechstroth, and Stephanie Tolan. *Guiding the Gifted Child.* Columbus, OH: Ohio Psychology Publishing Company, 1982.

Whitmore, Joanne R. "Discipline and the Gifted Child." *Roeper Review.* January, 1980. pp. 24-27.

Wright, L. *Parent Power: A Guide to Responsible Childrearing.* New York: William Morrow and Company, 1980.

NOW HEAR THIS!

The scene is a familiar one from the old situation comedy "The Honeymooners." Ralph is complaining to Alice that "you just don't listen to me anymore." The line is a setup for a quick-witted response from Alice. "Maybe if you had something to say worth listening to, Ralph . . ."

Jackie Gleason used comedy to express common problems in relationships. One of the reasons that "The Honeymooners" has enjoyed a delightful revival is that some of the problems in relationships and families are much the same today as they were in the 50s. One such problem is listening. Dianne R. Vertes, assistant professor of communication sciences at Case Western University, says that people of the 80s listen and comprehend less. She believes the "lazy listeners" among us are becoming an increasing problem.

A POP QUIZ FOR LAZY LISTENERS

True or False

As a Parent:

1. I value what my child has to say as much as what an adult has to say.

2. I listen with my eyes as well as my ears.

3. I limit "interior" noise when I listen.

4. I look for nonverbal communication clues from my child.

5. I have a "listening hobby" with my child.

6. I am an active listener more than a passive one.

Fill in the Blank

I have had _____ one-to-one conversations with my child in the last week. My child watches _____ hours of television each week.

Short Answer

List three communication tools that you use regularly to maintain good listening habits:

Explain: _____

_____

Essay

Define the words *listen* and *hear*. Compare or contrast the definitions with a recent example in your own life.

_____

_____

_____

Outline a positive and practical plan for improving active listening in your family.

_____

_____

_____

Well, how did you do? You be the teacher! Would you give yourself a passing grade? If several parents took the quiz, would the grades need to be on a curve? Could you hang your paper proudly on the refrigerator next to one of your child's papers? For those in need of a little remediation and review, read on.

ACTIVE LISTENING

Active listening is a way to be a tolerant, loving, and supportive parent. But it takes work—hard work! Hearing what someone else has just said can be a very passive event unless you process the information you receive in a way that makes you an active listener. By definition, to listen and to hear seem almost synonymous. However, most experts agree that listening and hearing are two separate activities. How well you listen, as a friend, a boss, an employee, or a parent, can be analyzed and, if need be, improved.

Techniques for Active Listeners

1. Limit distracting noise, both interior and exterior. External sounds, such as traffic, loud music, police sirens, screaming children, or machinery, can interfere with the listener's concentration. Interior noises, like worries, concerns, or being tired, can be just as distracting. Try to concentrate and tune out distractions. Example: After returning home from work, stop and unwind a few minutes. Change clothes, check the mail, pet the dog, or open a window. That slight "now I'm home" routine can help to empty the mind of interior noise and make it easier to listen, understand, and remember conversations with your family.

2. Avoid "mind battles" while listening. Mind battles occur when the listener starts arguing in his/her mind with what is being

said. The argument disrupts the continuity of the speaker's message. Try to suspend comment until the speaker is finished; then discuss your disagreements.

3. Use feedback during conversations. Ask the person speaking to repeat a point; then try to rephrase your answer. Ask questions. Keep asking until you "hit the nail on the head. " Examples: "Mary, it sounds like I am giving you too much hassle about getting good grades. Am I right?" "Could it be that you are expecting too much from yourself?" "I'm not sure I understand. Can you give me another example?" "Do you think I am using your accomplishments to make me feel like a better parent?"

4. Try to withhold judgements. If you are a critical parent, your child may become resistant and defensive just to prove that he/she, not you, has power over his/her life. Most important, try to create a safe environment for the child to vent frustrations, fears, anxieties, and disappoint- ments without endangering your relationship. It is much better to have an angry child screaming at you than an angry child sitting in silence screaming inside. Share your personal experiences during stressful conversations. If you trust your child with some of your personal pain, perhaps he/she will trust you with his/hers.

5. Look for and use nonverbal actions in listening. Good listeners use body language to improve communication. Eye contact is a must. Touching a shoulder, holding hands, or sitting close are all positive forms of communication. A listener with arms folded, a stiff back, and eyesfocused on the floor will surely guarantee a short, painful conversation.

6. Be a creative listener. There are many ways to listen. If "nose-to-nose" conversation is uncomfortable, use the telephone or ask the person to write you a note or letter. In the case of young children, use a puppet or toy as a listener. Good listeners use "tools" to help them feel more comfortable during conversations. Playing a simple card game can create a relaxed environment that stimulates conversation as well as listening.

7. Value what the speaker says, especially if the speaker is a child. Adults quite often don't pay attention to what children say. They hesitate to believe them. As a result, children find other ways to get adults to pay attention. Low grades, broken rules, and open rebellion are just a few of the ways that children might use to get adults to listen. "Listen now or pay later" might be practical advice to many parents. Let children know that their opinions count, even though you may not always agree.

8. Be a model. How you listen to other members of the family sets a powerful example for your child. Do other people think you are a good listener? Have you ever been told that you are a good listener? Can you be trusted with personal information? Can you keep a secret?

9. Shut off the TV! Television should not be your child's primary source of entertainment. It's not what is on television that is the big problem, it's what a child is missing when he/she is watching. According to research, the average child now watches 45 hours of television a week. That's a lot of missed conversations, walks in the park, fishing trips, ball games, and good books. For parents it means 45 hours of easy baby-sitting, 45 hours of quiet, passive children, and 45 hours of missed opportunities to listen—opportunities that are lost forever. Teachers now know why children get bored in school—they can't switch channels!

10. Choose a better time. Don't be afraid to admit that your're not in the mood to listen. Honesty is the best policy. Unless the topic is so important that it must be discussed immediately, many conversations can wait until the listener is more receptive. But always offer to listen later when your mind is more clear and your mood has improved.

CONCLUSION

A few weeks ago, while cleaning out a seldom-used closet, I discovered a very special box of memories—a time capsule of things once treasured by my grandmother. Among the scrapbooks, doilies, and photographs was one yellowed coloring book. Still identifiable on the cover were the words "Nancy and Grandma's Book 1950." As I looked through the carefully colored pages, images of my grandma and me flashed through my mind. You see, my grandma loved to color. Never alone, mind you. She loved to color with me, just me—her favorite grandchild. (At least she made me think I was her favorite.) That made one little girl feel very special. Not only did my grandma love to color, but she also loved to listen to me talk. (At least, she made me think that she did.) We would color and talk for hours. Actually, we would both do the coloring, but I did most of the talking! As an only child, I can remember how much I looked forward to visiting with my grandma. I never went without a coloring book, crayons, and lots of stuff to talk about. In fact,

I would save up things, special things, just to tell Grandma. I told her everything. She would ask questions now and then and tell a story once in awhile, but mostly she just listened.

At the bottom of the box of memories was a stack of letters that my grandmother had written to my uncle who was in the Air Force at the time. As a I glanced through one of the letters, my eyes were drawn to a postscript that read: "I have to close now, Ed. Nancy is running up the drive. I have to catch up on a little listening."

FATHERS ARE PEOPLE TOO!

A Very Special Owner's Manual

Some people call it pride; others call it just plain stubbornness. Whatever the situation, most people rely on their experiences and innate abilities to pull them through. However, there comes a time when we all reach the breaking point of frustration and remember that time-honored bit of philosophy: WHEN ALL ELSE FAILS—READ THE DIRECTIONS!

A case in point:

I had saved up a lot of time, anxiety, and money for that day. A new car must surely be the ultimate adult toy. When the dealer handed me the keys along with the owner's manual, my insides began to jiggle with excitement.

I promptly placed the key in the ignition and tossed the manual into the glove box. Away I went! A few miles later, my new digital dashboard began flashing a message to me that car dealers not only offer low interest rates, but also low gas tanks.

Not to worry. I pulled into a local service station still smiling and still jiggling inside. Fifteen minutes later the jiggling had turned to a cement made of anger and frustration. I couldn't get to the gas cap because the metal hinged cover was stuck or locked or SOMETHING!

Would you believe I couldn't figure out how to put gas in the car? I pushed, pulled, turned, and twisted every button, lever, and handle in that car, and the cover over the gas cap still would not budge.

In fifteen minutes I had managed to turn on the radio, the windshield wipers, the heater, the headlights, taillights, courtesy lights, and the map-reading light. The radio antenna went up and the power seats went down. The trunk unlocked and the doors locked. The side mirrors tilted to the left, while the turn signals flashed on the right.

Now wait a minute! As the anger built, I began to talk to myself. I'm an adult, right? I should be able to figure this out, right? I mean, really! Seven years of college and two degrees must be good for something. It would be too embarrassing to ask for help, right? WRONG. When the radio spit a cassette tape at me, I knew the end was near.

In desperation I reached for the owner's manual. Of course, I found the answer. (A small yellow button in the glove box did the trick.) However, what was more important, and the point of this whole story, was all the useful information I learned while looking for the answer to my problem.

Owner's manuals, I found out, are fascinating documents, filled with important information. And my new car will probably survive its owner much longer because I took the time to . . .

READ THE DIRECTIONS!

Even though sons and daughters should never be considered possessions, there are times when parents everywhere wished their children had been born with an owner's manual in one hand and an operator's guide in the other. Hopefully the analogy that follows will be fun as well as helpful for all those parents who are struggling with gifted children.

SECTION I: BEFORE DRIVING YOUR VEHICLE

Your new vehicle does not need an extensive break-in. It should be ready to go on the day of purchase. Try not to drive continuously at the same speed, as parts tend to adjust themselves better to other parts if various speeds are used during the first 1,000 miles. You should read the Warranty Information Booklet carefully. It contains a basic statement of your rights and responsibilities.

It's true. Most babies are ready to go from day One. Traditionally, fathers had a little more time to adjust to the new humans in their lives because mothers were the primary caretakers of children. No more! Fathers everywhere are accepting their responsibilities and rights in parenting their children. Dr. Ross Parke, University of Illinois psychologist, says that fathers are just as competent as mothers at parenting. Many other researchers are quick to agree. Through their special kind of play, fathers provide children with important and invaluable social skills. *Men's Health*, a Rodale Press Publication, explains several important aspects of play:

1. The popularity of three-year-old children with their playmates, as rated by their teachers, is significantly correlated to healthy play with their fathers. The better the father is at physical play—the more he allows the child to dictate the tempo of play and the more responsive the two of them are to each other—the more popular and socially at ease the child is with other children.

2. The father's style of play, it seems, provides a safe setting for children to learn how to express positive emotions,

how to recognize other people's emotions, and how to send their own signals.

3. In a study of infant-care skills, fathers were found to be as competent as mothers at noticing changes in their babies behaviors and modifying their own behaviors in response.

4. Mothers are more likely to use toys with the babies and to try to teach through play; they also engage in more verbal and watching games. Fathers tend to favor more physical play, bouncing and lifting the babies more than mothers.

It seems clear that as a society we are moving away from the tradition of mothers being the primary caretakers of children. Fathers are taking their place, and rightfully so, in the mainstream of child care.

Because gifted children quite often walk and talk early, the need for fathers to become involved as caretakers is even more important.

SECTION II: GETTING TO KNOW YOUR VEHICLE

The vehicle identification number is stamped on a metal tag near the bottom of the windshield. It is visible from outside the vehicle. Each identification number is unique to that vehicle.

Your child is unique. There has never been a human quite like your son or daughter and there will never be another. Getting to know your child takes time, lots of time. There is an overabundance of reading about the importance of "quality time" between parents and children. Some so-called experts maintain it isn't how much time a parent spends with a child but rather how the time is spent. Hogwash! Time is time. You either have it or you don't. A short time is a short time. You can't get to know your child by spending a few minutes of "quality time" with him/her.

It takes TIME to:

- Walk hand in hand through the park.
- Drive thirty miles to dance lessons.
- Shut off the TV and have a quiet conversation.
- Plan ahead with something special in mind for your child.
- Put a puzzle together.
- Read to your child every day.
- Join a parent support group for gifted children.
- Write special notes to your child.
- Stop and answer one more question.
- Renegotiate an allowance.
- Go shopping for new clothes.
- Surprise your child by showing up for lunch at school.
- Go with your child rather than sending him/her.
- Help your child fix supper.
- Attend a music recital.
- Get to know your child's friends.
- Teach your daughter how to fish.
- Teach your son to macrame.
- Have a mud fight in the backyard.
- Learn a new skill yourself just so you can teach it to your child.
- Play.
- Sing.
- Cry.
- Laugh.
- Make time.

SECTION III: OPERATING YOUR VEHICLE

There are two important factors you can control to improve fuel economy: the mechanical condition of your vehicle and how well you drive it. A well-tuned, properly maintained vehicle will deliver better economy than a neglected vehicle. To be sure your vehicle is in top operating condition, avoid long periods of idling, do not drive with your foot resting on the brake pedal, and look ahead and anticipate changing traffic conditions.

A slightly different way of "relaxing the spirit" is hobbies. Fathers who have hobbies are providing good models for their children. If a father is too busy to have a hobby, a gifted son or daughter might feel guilty for having one. Hobbies, as well as other extra-curricular activities, play a significant role in the career choices of children. Parents should provide opportunities for their children to learn about the many careers that are available now or that might be developed in the future. WARNING: The parents' role should be one of a guide, adviser, and friend; but the final choice must be left to the child. Preparing your child to look ahead and anticipate the future can begin with a few simple ideas:

1. Give your gifted child responsibilities at home. When you do, you are sending a strong message that you think he/she is a competent person.

2. Respect your child's ideas. Children can have very strong opinions about things. You may not agree, but at least listen to their thoughts and feelings.

3. Give your child choices rather than ultimatums. Life as an adult consists of making one choice after another. You can never start too early in giving your child practice in this important life skill. For example, giving a child the choice of bathing before or after a favorite TV program is better than the ultimatum, "Go take your bath right now, or else!"

4. As your child reaches puberty, be prepared to accept "safe" rebellion. This can be particularly difficult for fathers. But stop and think about it. Which would be better—a punk hairdo or illegal drugs? When you get right down to it, Dad, maybe a few years of looking at purple hair isn't so bad after all!

5. Don't be afraid to tell those "I walked two miles to school in the snow" stories. There might be a groan or two at first, but children really do like to hear about the good old days (even if it was only 1962). Children need to be reassured that other people, especially parents, know what they are feeling.

6. Encourage the **same** options for daughters as for sons. For example, computer equity is a problem for girls in our public schools. They seem to be falling behind in math and science just as they did in the late 50s and early 60s. The reason is attitude. Of course, the same attitude problem can occur

73

with boys. Dad, will you laugh at your son if he shows an interest in taking a home economics class?

7. Give your child a break from school and take him/her to work with you. This has been a tradition in Russia for years. The Russian government wants Soviet children to respect work and be proud of what their parents do.

8. Encourage your children to develop an interest in a passionate cause. Whether it is a campaign to save the whales or elect a favorite politician, children need to know that what they do can make a difference. Begin by helping your child write a letter to an influential person concerning his/her cause.

9. Practice several "try and fail" maneuvers in front of your son or daughter. Parents are the very best teachers of "if at first you don't succeed, try, try again." Gifted children have a way of exaggerating problems to the point that a sense of hopelessness takes over. Help them to analyze the situation. How bad is the situation?

10. Establish father/son and father/daughter traditions in your family. For example, my father and I collected pine branches every Christmas for my mother to make into wreaths. The trip to the pine forest was talked about and carefully planned every year. Such traditions create a special kind of security in a family. Perhaps there were traditions that you participated in with your parents or grandparents. It is important to carry on such traditions with your own children. If you can't remember any, start some new ones.

CONCLUSION

Well, we only scratched the surface. The owner's manual for any car has a lot more neat ideas, and the manual on raising children will probably never be finished. My favorite page in the car manual is on page one. It says, "Today, more than ever, the cars and trucks of this motor company are being built with pride. We believe this pride of workmanship will, in turn, provide you with pride of ownership." That's it. Pride. It's another form of love for fathers everywhere. Remember how you felt, Dad, when the nurse or doctor announced the birth of your child? It's a boy! It's a girl! Remember that feeling? Didn't it make you feel good? Sort of makes you jiggle inside now, doesn't it?

RESOURCES

Ehrlich, Virginia Z. *Gifted Children, A Guide for Parents and Teachers*. New York: Trillium Press, 1985.

"Gifted Children Newsletter," Vol. 5, No. 9. September, 1984.

Owner Guide. 1986 Mercury Cougar, Ford Motor Company. Copyright 1985.

GIFTED CHILDREN AT RISK

The following are excerpts from *A Nation at Risk*, a report by The National Commission on Excellence in Education:

... over half the population of gifted students do not match their tested ability with comparable achievement in school.

... the most gifted students may need a curriculum enriched and accelerated beyond even the needs of other students of high ability.

... if necessary, additional time should be found to meet the special needs of slow learners, the gifted, and others who need more instructional diversity than can be accommodated during a conventional school day or school year.

... placement and grouping of students, as well as promotion and graduation policies, should be guided by the academic process of students and their instructional needs rather than by a rigid adherence to age.

... the Federal Government, in cooperation with states and localities, should help meet the needs of key groups of students such as the gifted and talented, the socio-economically disadvantaged, minority and language minority students, and the handicapped. In combination, these groups include both national resources and the Nation's youth who are **most at risk**.

... our goal must be to develop the talents of all to their fullest. Attaining that goal requires that we expect and assist all students to work to the limits of their capabilities. We should expect schools to have genuinely high standards rather than minimum ones, and we should expect parents to support and encourage their children to make the most of their talents and abilities.

GIFTED EDUCATION: A TOOL FOR EXCELLENCE

Administrators often ask why they should take the time to become involved in programming for gifted children. They have that "Why should we bother?" look in their eyes. Of course, an advocate of gifted education would quickly respond by saying, "Because gifted children deserve it!" But in recent years, we have discovered some interesting and exciting fringe benefits of gifted programs. For lack of a better term, it can be called the *spill over effect*. What happens is this: as school districts examine what to do for gifted children, they begin to instruct their teachers in new and innovative teaching methods. As teachers are taught how to improve their technique with gifted children, something "spills over," and all children are touched. In effect, the education of all children is improved by improving the education of just a few.

Good teaching is not the only benefit of gifted programs. The curriculum comes under close scrutiny when gifted programs are being considered. A curriculum that stimulates high-level thinking is vital for gifted children. When the present curriculum doesn't provide enough such activities, it is changed or modified. In the process, the entire curriculum is examined, and the improvements for gifted children result in improvements for **all** children.

So, in response to that "Why should we bother?" look: To make teachers better teachers, **get involved in gifted education**. It will pull from teachers the best they have to offer children. Gifted children demand excellence from educators! And to improve the curriculum, **get involved in gifted education.** Adding and/or changing learning activities to stimulate high-level thinking will force the curriculum to move from adequate to excellent.

76

Yes, we should bother. Excellence for the sake of gifted children brings the chance for excellence for **all.**

EXCELLENCE COSTS MONEY

Parents, your gifted children deserve the best education that money can buy. However, we must improve the public's attitude toward education if we are ever to see adequate funding for gifted programs. In America, we spend an estimated 20 billion dollars annually on cigarettes and cigars but only half a billion on textbooks for our children. As taxpayers, parents have the right and the responsibility to see that their tax dollars are spent wisely.

PAY ATTENTION! Do you know what decisions are being made by your local school district concerning how state and federal monies are being spent?

MONITOR! Are you aware of the activities of your local school board? Do you visit school **often** to observe what your children are being taught and how?

SPEAK UP! If you agree with what is happening for your children, you **must** send a letter of support to your child's teacher, principal, and school board. Have you? If you disagree, you must try to influence educational policy by voicing your concern and demanding that changes be made. Have you?

Too many parents pay their school taxes and then sit back as though they have fulfilled their responsibility. Excellence in education will be a reality when we all accept the responsibility for it. Exactly how much will it cost? Locked up in the minds of gifted children are the cures, the answers, and the hopes for the future. Can we put a price tag on that?

EXCELLENCE BEGINS AT HOME

The research has shown time and again that students who come from homes where learning is a lifelong process and knowledge is respected are consistently higher achievers. If gifted children are exposed to models (parents) who consistently strive toward excellence, they, too, will expect excellence from themselves and others. The few hours a day your child spends in school can hardly compare with the strong impressions he/she receives at home. As parents, you can recommit yourselves to a love of learning, a respect for education, and a need for self-improvement.

EXCELLENT SOLUTIONS: A RISKY BUSINESS

If the nation's gifted children are truly at risk as the report indicates, then the solutions to the problem are surely risky. Those looking for easy solutions need look no further. History has taught us our fascination with easy solutions has hardly ever led to a real answer. Yes, merit pay, longer school days, and tougher standards are all alternatives worth considering; but will they really solve the problem or just treat the symptoms?

As we search for solutions, let us not forget all those teachers, administrators, and parents who have **always** been in search of excellence in education, who have been taking risks for years to see that our children received the best education **they** had the power to provide, and who didn't wait for a federal grant, a memo from the superintendent, or a report from a commission to demand excellence in themselves. Is it possible that we already have excellence in education? Perhaps the solution is to learn what we already know.

IT'S ONLY JARGON

A Dictionary for Parents

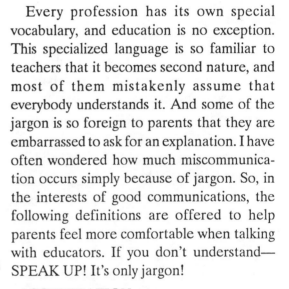

There are many useful definitions for the jargon that teachers and consultants use in gifted education. But, when parents read written reports concerning their children's progress or participate in conferences with teachers they must feel like they are listening to a foreign language.

Every profession has its own special vocabulary, and education is no exception. This specialized language is so familiar to teachers that it becomes second nature, and most of them mistakenly assume that everybody understands it. And some of the jargon is so foreign to parents that they are embarrassed to ask for an explanation. I have often wondered how much miscommunication occurs simply because of jargon. So, in the interests of good communications, the following definitions are offered to help parents feel more comfortable when talking with educators. If you don't understand—SPEAK UP! It's only jargon!

ACCELERATION

covering the curriculum at a fast pace. Most gifted children need a shorter time to learn new things. By accelerating the curriculum, we eliminate replication and excess drill. On rare occasions the child is accelerated (skips a grade) instead of the curriculum.

ACCOUNTABILITY

the demand for proof that your child's school is meeting its obligations to educate gifted children.

ACCOUNTANT

a man or woman you hire to figure out how you are going to pay for your gifted child's music lessons, summer camp, computer, encyclopedias, or college education!

ACHIEVEMENT TESTS

instruments that measure what your child knows academically and what he/she can do academically; for example, California Achievement Test, Scholastic Aptitude Test (SAT), American College Test (ACT). These tests reveal strengths and weaknesses in your child's academic abilities. They should also help educators improve instruction, aid in forming goals and objectives for the curriculum, and determine content and skills.

BINET, ALFRED (1857-1911)

a French psychologist who, along with Theodore Simon, developed the first useful test of a child's intelligence. Lewis Terman (1905) adapted the Binet-Simon Test to the American student and later, while teaching at Stanford University, revised it. The new test was titled the Stanford-Binet Test. It is widely considered to be one of the best individual I Q tests available. The test has been revised several times.

BRAINSTORMING

a group activity that stimulates creative and high-level thinking. The word itself was developed and named by Alex Osborne, an advertising executive. Children are usually given a topic and asked to come up with as many ideas related to that topic as possible. All ideas are accepted without criticism. Brainstorming is designed to generate creative ideas with no right or wrong answers. It is the basis for many activities involving gifted children.

CHANGE AGENT

what you can be if there is no gifted program in your child's school. Ronald Havelock says there are four functions that a change agent can perform: (1) disrupt the status quo, (2) offer solutions, (3) provide resource help, and (4) match resource people with problems to be solved. You can do it!

COMPACT

to cover the same amount of materials or activities in less time by allowing more time for enrichment activities and projects better suited to in dividual interest and needs.

COMPUTER

an electronic machine which, by means of stored instructions and information, performs rapid, often complex calculations. A machine which every gifted child should own.

CONVERGENT THINKING

focusing on one particular answer. Convergent thinking or production is one of the elements found in Dr. J.P. Guilford's research model of the Structure of Intellect. Divergent thinking focuses on many answers. Convergent thinking focuses on a single answer, Most intelligence tests require convergent thinking.

CREATIVITY

a complex mental process that is very difficult to define. Creativity is more than the ability to draw well as many people believe.

It involves putting together new, different, and unique ideas. It is found in all children to a certain degree. Creative thinking can be used in all content areas not just art. Some of the experts in the field include J.W. Getzels, P. Jackson, J.P. Guilford, E. Paul Torrance, and Frank Williams.

DIFFERENTIATED CURRICULUM

a set of activities, a program, or a plan of instruction that is designed to meet the unique needs of special children. Gifted children may not deserve more than other children in our public schools, but they do deserve different. "Different" for gifted children means a curriculum that allows for acceleration, stimulation of high-level thinking, divergent thinking, and convergent thinking.

DIVERGENT THINKING

another element of J.P. Guilford's research model for the Structure of Intellect. Your gifted child is doing divergent thinking when he/she comes up with new and unique ideas about things. The ideas may not always be practical. In many ways, divergent thinking is the opposite of convergent thinking.

DRILL

the repetition of a skill to reinforce what has already been learned. Commonly referred to as practice! Commonly referred to by gifted kids as "boring"!

ENRICHMENT PROGRAMS

learning activities that go beyond the regular curricular activities. John Gowan and George Demos in *The Education and Guidance of the Ablest,* (Springfield, IL: Charles C. Thomas, Publisher, 1964) suggested that enrichment programs will be successful if the student (1) is encouraged to search for new information, (2) is provided with leadership opportunities, (3) is able to pursue personal interests, (4) is able to engage in creative assignments, (5) can develop his/her own initiative, and (6) engages in in-depth activities that are, in fact, broadening. Enrichment programs usually take the form of special classes or special schools for the gifted. They might also involve itinerant teachers who provide regular classroom teachers with help for their gifted students. These special teachers might also pull out the gifted students from the regular classroom in order to involve them in special activities.

EVALUATION

to make judgments about the value or worth of something. Just about anything can be evaluated: a person, an object, a happening, an organization, or a program. Usually a set of criteria in the form of a checklist is used to evaluate a gifted program. Quite often this checklist is given to parents as well as educators and students. Evaluations of gifted students themselves might take the form of tests, group discussions, or self-evaluation. Evaluation does not always mean grading. It is most important to remember that the real purpose of evaluation is to provide information so the person, object, happening, or-

ganization, or program might be changed, adapted, improved, or accepted as is.

HIGH-LEVEL THINKING

emphasizes tasks and activities that involve (1) analysis, synthesis, and evaluation, (2) viewing situations from various perspectives, (3) finding several "layers of meaning" by using metaphors, analogies, paradoxes, and (4) generating different possible solutions by showing fluency, flexibility, originality, and elaboration of thought.

HONORS PROGRAMS

courses or programs offered in high schools and colleges for high achievers. These courses are usually planned to motivate the intellectually gifted learner. The content is broader, the curriculum accelerated, and the instructor carefully selected. In some cases, high school students who complete an honors program receive college credit for their efforts.

IMAGERY

mental images or pictures as produced by memory or imagination. Educators are learning the importance of teaching children how to visualize; that is, how to create images in their minds. One such method now being used in many classrooms is guided fantasy. The children close their eyes and try to create images that have been stimulated by a story or poem the teacher is reading. After the fantasy, the children are usually asked to tell, write, or draw about what they have imaged.

INDEPENDENT STUDY

a self-directed style of learning. Usually independent study is done with the help of a teacher. However, the role of the teacher is limited. The students complete various activities on their own time. One important goal of independent study is to teach children that there are several ways to gather information and learn things. Some gifted students have become locked into a "book-learning" mode. An in-depth independent study program will stretch the gifted students into discovering new ways of researching an idea; for example, conducting interviews, viewing films, or writing letters to authorities related to topic.

MENTOR

a friend, wise adviser, and teacher. A mentor is a person in the community who is willing to spend time with gifted children, listen to their problems, share opinions, and give advice. If the mentor is also gifted, the benefits are even more meaningful to the gifted children. (See SELF-ESTEEM.)

PATIENCE

ability to wait or endure; specifically, to deal with gifted children with calmness and self-control!

PEER TUTORING

a program in which students teach other students. When older children tutor younger children, it is usually referred to as cross-age tutoring. It can be an emotionally gratifying experience for gifted children to teach. However, parents should be on the lookout for signs that peer tutoring is being overdone. Peer tutoring should never be used as a substitute for teacher instruction.

POST HOLING

encouraging investigation of subjects, ideas, or problems in depth rather than surveying a variety of topics. Gifted children should always be encouraged to dig a little deeper as they research a topic.

PROBLEM SOLVING METHOD

defined by the National Council of Supervisors of Mathematics as "the process of applying previously acquired knowledge to new and unfamiliar situations." Many teachers of the gifted devote large amounts of time to the formal teaching of problem solving. The method may involve researching a specific problem, analyzing various situations, participating in group discussions and simulation games, evaluating, and following up. In some school districts, teams of "problem solvers" compete with teams from other districts. The goal of each team is to attend the National Future Problem Solving Bowl.

RISK TAKER

not afraid of failure, willing to take chances in order to learn new things. Many gifted children are perfectionists and do not like to get involved in new activities unless they know or believe they can do it easily and correctly. Unfortunately, some gifted children learn to be average in school because they have never learned to be risk takers. An important goal of many gifted programs is to provide opportunities for risk taking; for example, leadership activities, creative problem solving programs, or simulation games.

SELF-ESTEEM

a feeling about one's self-worth or self-concept. A positive self-image is the key to success for most people—children included. When gifted children lack confidence in their own abilities, no amount of outside motivation will turn them into high achievers. Students with a high self-esteem believe in themselves. High achievement and high self-esteem go hand in hand.

TAXONOMY

a step-by-step approach to classifying a group of things. In this case, we are talking about Bloom's Taxonomy. Hundreds of gifted programs in this country use Bloom's Taxonomy as a model for developing curriculum for gifted children. Benjamin S. Bloom, along with others, developed the taxonomy for educational objectives in 1956. Learning is divided into three parts or domains: cognitive, affective, and psychomotor. Each domain is then divided . For example, the cognitive domain is broken down into activities involving knowledge, comprehension, application, analysis, synthesis, and evaluation. Application, analysis, synthesis, and evaluation are considered high-level thinking.

RESOURCES

Bloom, Benjamin S. et al., eds. *Taxonomy of Educational Objectives: Handbook I*. New York: David McKay Company, Inc., 1976.

Dejnorzka, Edward L., and David E. Kapel, eds. *American Educators' Encyclopedia*. Westport, CT: Greenwood Press, 1982.

Kluwe, Rainer H., and Hans Spada. *Developmental Models of Thinking*. New York: Academic Press, 1980.

Passow, A. Harry, ed. *The Gifted and the Talented: Their Education and Development* (NSSE 78th Yearbook, Part I). Chicago: University of Chicago Press, 1979.

Putnam, John F, and W. Dale Chrismore, eds. *Standard Terminology for Curriculum and Instruction in Local and State School Systems* (State Educational Records and Reports Series: Handbook VI). Washington, DC: National Center for Education Statistics, U.S. Department 01, Health, Education, and Welfare, 1970.

GIFTED ON TUESDAYS

There is no doubt about it! The best place to find out what is going on in a school is the teachers' lounge. Not long ago, a wandering education consultant stopped by such a fountain of information on her way to a teacher in-service workshop. After a few polite introductions, she asked what was happening for gifted children in that particular school. The most experienced teacher described the situation with much confidence.

"Oh yes," she said. "We have a gifted program here. We have a coordinator and everything. Her name is Bertha . . . something or other. She comes in here every Tuesday and takes the gifted kids into the library for class. I don't know what she does with them in there, but whatever it is, she does it every Tuesday. Just like clockwork, every Tuesday. Yes sir, we have gifted education covered in this building. No problem!" They're gifted all right—every Tuesday!

Our wandering consultant wasn't surprised at the teacher's explanation. Such a response is becoming quite common. In all fairness to the teacher, she was simply treating the gifted program the same way she might treat the speech correction program. If a classroom teacher has a student who exhibits speech problems, it is customary to call the speech teacher to take care of it.

After all, the speech teacher is a specialist and much more qualified to handle the child's needs. It is understandable how the same psychology can be applied to gifted education. If a classroom teacher is having problems with a gifted child, the coordinator of the gifted program or the teacher of the gifted (if there is one) is called to deal with the situation.

The word is OWNERSHIP. And in some gifted programs there isn't much. It may sound like splitting hairs, but there is a difference between the terms gifted *program* and gifted *education*. A gifted program may be the job and/or responsibility of just a few people—a coordinator, an administrator, and designated teachers. Gifted education, on the other hand, is everyone's job. Administrators, teachers, parents, and citizens in the community must take ownership of gifted education by accepting the responsibility for the future of our gifted children.

Don't misunderstand. We need gifted programs. We need coordinators. We need teachers of the gifted. Many school districts have worked years to develop such programs.

However, many gifted programs are stuck in a rut—they are stuck on Tuesdays. Parents may be the best hope for pulling gifted programs out of the "Tuesday rut" and into a comprehensive, articulated attempt at gifted education. Parents can help monitor their gifted child's education by comparing the services provided by the gifted program with the needs of their child.

SPECIAL NEEDS OF THE GIFTED

Dr. J. F. Feldhusen in the *Journal for the Education of the Gifted*, Summer 1983, states that gifted students have a number of special needs, such as the following:

● Maximum achievement of basic skills and concepts.

● Learning activities at the appropriate level and pace.

● Experience in creative thinking and problem solving.

● Development of convergent abilities, especially in logical deduction and problem solving.

● Stimulation of imagery, imagination, and spatial abilities.

● Development of self-awareness and acceptance of own capabilities, interests, and needs.

● Stimulation to pursue higher level goals and aspirations (models, pressure, standards).

● Development of independence, self-direction, and discipline in learning.

● Experience in relating intellectually, artistically, and affectively with other gifted, creative, and/or talented students.

● A large fund of information about diverse topics.

● Exposure to a variety of fields of study, to art, and to information about professions and occupations.

- Access to reading material and stimulation to take advantage of it.

POSSIBLE SERVICES TO CHILDREN

Dr. Feldhusen also states that a variety of services are needed to meet those needs. The following is a list of possible services that can be offered at the elementary, junior high/middle school, or secondary level.

- Accelerated classes
- Correspondence courses
- Upgraded or multi-age classrooms
- Continuous progress
- Cluster grouping within the regular classroom
- Special full-time classes for the gifted
- Pullout classes
- Part-time groups meeting before and after school or on Saturdays
- Schools for the gifted
- Resource rooms
- Demonstration centers
- Counseling
- Junior Great Books
- Future Problem Solving
- Advanced placement classes
- Odyssey of the Mind
- Talents Unlimited
- Mathcounts
- Writing across the content areas
- Johns Hopkins Math/Writing Talent Search
- Seminars
- Mentors
- Career exploration

- Independent study
- College classes
- Proficiency testing
- Honors classes
- Foreign language study
- Classes in logic, leadership, creativity, psychology, humanities, law, music, political science, research

The list is exciting and it's growing. The number of services a school district offers gifted children can often be measured by the strength of its parent support group. In many school districts, half of the services to gifted children are provided by parent volunteers.

QUESTIONS

Following is a list of questions that parents might ask administrators, teachers, and/or school board members concerning gifted education. The questions you choose to ask, when you ask them, and how you ask them can make a difference between establishing yourself as a supportive, concerned parent or a pushy, problem parent.

1. What are my legal rights in respect to adequate programming for my gifted child? Is gifted education mandated in this state?

2. Does our school board have a policy statement concerning gifted children?

3. How much funding is set aside each year for the education of gifted children? How much is that compared to the funding of other areas of special education; for example deaf, blind, mentally retarded?

4. Are special workshops, seminars, or classes related to the needs of gifted children being offered in our district for teachers and administrators?

5. Are students permitted to "proficiency out" of certain classes?

6. Are students permitted to accelerate by skipping grades?

7. What is the school's policy concerning individual I.Q. testing for gifted students?

8. Are there gifted programs in other school districts that I could visit?

9. How can I help to support this district's gifted program? Can I volunteer my services to improve the program?

10. What is the district's hiring policy concerning new teachers? Is the district looking for talented teachers who are deeply committed to serve and inspire gifted children?

11. Are teachers, administrators, parents, school board members, and other citizens in the community encouraged and allowed to attend conferences or state/regional/national conventions related to gifted education?

12. Are specific classes in gifted education being offered at a local college or university?

13. What is the name of the state director for gifted education?

14. Can you recommend any books, journals, or periodicals that might help me improve my parenting skills?

15. What are the names and addresses of my state and federal legislators? Which ones support gifted education?

16. Is there a state or local parent support group for gifted education? How can I join?

17. When is the next school board meeting?

GIFTED EDUCATION: IT'S COME A LONG WAY — OR HAS IT?

Many school districts are taking a second look at their gifted programs. They are seeking innovative approaches. The latest terms being bounced around are *infusion* and *integration*. That is, making the gifted program part of the regular classroom. Districts are finally finding out that gifted children are not just gifted on Tuesdays. The "Tuesday rut" is producing gifted children who don't want to be gifted and who feel isolated, misunderstood, and put down. The "Tuesday rut" is letting some teachers, parents, and administrators off the hook of responsibility. What is needed are "Tuesday" programs that are part of an extensive gifted education plan. Forcing gifted children to hold back their giftedness every day but Tuesday is unfair, cruel, and even illegal in more and more states.

Hmmmmm . . . I wonder if Thomas Edison invented the light bulb on a Tuesday?

TEXTBOOK DEPENDENCY

A TRADITIONAL CONSPIRACY

Educators have learned that the path of least resistance in the classroom is the ever present, ever faithful TEXTBOOK! If an educator broke away from this traditional time honored teaching tool, waves of guilt usually followed. There always seemed to be plenty of fuel for the fire from parents and other educators in support of textbooks:

- "Those books were good enough for me when I was in school, so by golly they're good enough now."

- "Just stick to the textbook, Deary, and you can't go wrong."

- "Let's cut all the frills, just buy the basic textbooks for the kids and a manual for the teacher."

And the favorite:

- "We've tried all that creativity, finger painting, touchy, feely nonsense; it's time to get back to the basics."

And the beat goes on and on; the result is a conspiracy. Who's involved in the conspiracy? Teachers, parents, administrators, school board members—just about everybody who is involved in educating children. However, teachers seem to get blamed first when the conspiracy is exposed. Defectors from the textbook conspiracy risk ridicule, ostracism, or even dismissal from their jobs. No wonder many give up the fight and return to the trenches armed with a new set of textbooks. Some educators spend their entire careers searching for that special, perfect textbook with all the magic answers.

TO THE TEACHER

Not all textbooks are bad. When textbooks are used as part of a curriculum, acting as organizational aids, discussion starters, or sources of factual information, they serve a purpose. But when they are used as a whole program, they encourage passivity and block inquiry because **they teach answers, not questions**" (Vair, *Independent School*, December 1981). Textbooks are pre-digested materials that force the learner into a passive absorption of information and a blind acceptance of someone else's opinion. For a teacher, a constant "stick to the textbook curriculum" discourages initiative and frustrates creativity. Children who are taught by passive, answer-giving, fact-finding, textbook teachers, emulate that style in their own learning. Is that the model we want for our students?

In *Gifted Children: Reaching Their Potential* (New York: Trillium Press, 1979), psychologist Paul Torrance wrote, "When we asked our gifted young people for their perceptions of the future world of work they frequently list teaching as one of the occupations most likely to become obsolete within the next 25 years . . . What gifted students seem to be saying is that what most teachers do (dispense information) can be done more accurately, efficiently, and economically by computers and other technology . . . All of this has convinced me that we must conceptualize and articulate a new image of teaching."

TO PARENTS

There are many teachers out there in the trenches trying to articulate a new image of teaching. They need your support. They need your POWER. One concerned parent to a school board is worth ten concerned teachers. Not only do you have the responsibility to support your child's school, you have the POWER to determine what choices and opportunities your child will have.

TO ALL CO-CONSPIRATORS

A curriculum filled with imagination, originality, and experimentation, or a curriculum filled only with textbooks. Which will it be? Should a child's future as an adult be determined only by test scores and grades for the RIGHT ANSWERS, or by an education based on imagining, exploring ideas, encouraging original thought, and ASKING QUESTIONS rather than answering them?

SARAH'S SCHOOL

Home Schooling: A Choice for the 90s?

Her name is Sarah and she is my friend. She is a delightful, precocious six-year-old with long silky hair and a soft smile. She has a gentle nature, and a sincere, almost intense caring for other human beings. Her dreams include being an astronaut and managing a center for lonely people. She's a talker! Her sharp memory provides the basis for long conversations about people she has met and places she has been.

Is she gifted? Probably. She is reading and doing math at several grade levels above her age peers. She lives with her parents and baby brother in a large restored home built in 1869 in Chatham, Virginia. This beautiful Victorian house has been home to the Mitchell family since 1975. This big white house on Whittle Street is steeped in history. Legend has it that the home was once part of the "pot" in a poker game. But now there is new history being made in the old home: Henry and Patricia Mitchell have decided to keep their children out of public school. Sarah has developed her social, emotional, and intellectual abilities in a home-school situation. The Mitchells are one of only two families in their county who have chosen home schooling.

Is it working? In Sarah's case, the answer is "yes." Sarah's school is like a giant wheel that covers the world. The hub of the wheel is the Mitchell kitchen. It's a warm, friendly place with a high ceiling, shelves full of books, walls covered with pictures and maps, and a floor cluttered with toys, a baby brother, and a cat named Sugar Whiskers. Most of Sarah's "book learning" takes place here.

She begins her day by choosing from the many commercial materials her parents have gathered. She is currently doing some of her math in a fourth-grade text. She particularly enjoys reading and is a frequent visitor to the local library.

However, Sarah's classroom quickly begins to expand with trips to the post office and grocery store. Patricia Mitchell turns simple family outings into learning experiences. Sarah is quick to confess that one of her favorite people is the produce man at the local grocery store!

The spokes of the wheel take Sarah in many different directions. Some are short, to the backyard and the garden. Others extend as far away as Paris, France. Sarah has traveled to several foreign countries with her parents and grandmother. Every trip is another classroom, another learning experience, another set of memories. The wheel is always turning, changing direction, growing larger. As Sarah grows and changes, her needs will change, and so will the wheel. Henry and Patricia Mitchell are always planning new experiences for their family. The education of their children has become a priority in their lives.

Will home schooling work for all children? Probably not. Few parents would be willing to put the time into educating their own children. Patricia Mitchell is very quick to proclaim that home schooling is a FULL-TIME JOB! However, more and more parents are accepting the challenges and the demands of home schooling. Over 35 states now permit home schooling by law under various conditions.

Some states rule by policy or court decisions rather than by law. Few states, if any, make it easy for parents to educate their children at home. The reasons vary, but most are centered around the concerns of professional educators who are convinced that parents practicing home schooling have neither the patience nor the proper training to handle an acceptable curriculum for their children. They are also concerned with documentation and evaluation.

Some experts disagree. Raymond Moore, author of *School Can Wait*, maintains that on standard tests, home-schooed children outperform students educated traditionally. He says they also receive better grades when they go back to school. He believes nearly all go on to college and credits parental tutelage with their success. (*U. S. News & World Report*, Sept. 22, 1981)

John Hold, editor of the monthly newsletter, *Growing Without Schooling,* says, "Schools are not only destructive of intellect but character. With very few exceptions, the social life of our schools is mean-spirited, competitive, status-seeking, snobbish, cruel, and often violent."

Probably the biggest concern that educators have is the one expressed by John Morgan, a principal from Illinois, who worries about a child's social development. "Children learn from other people not just one teacher. How can a child educated at home really compare socially with one educated in a group?"

Henry and Patricia Mitchell do not believe that home schooling hinders their child's social development. The Mitchells answered the socialization question in a recent article that appeared in the *Star-Tribune*, Chatham, Virginia. "We feel the home school can do far better in this area than the institutional school. First, the artificial age-level grouping found in a school does not prepare a student for interaction with people of all ages in the real world. Learning in the home and community environment does.

Second, the regimentation and enforced military silence necessary to control large school groups does not leave much opportunity for meaningful conversation and interaction. Third, there is a negative aspect to the constant interaction of many youngsters of the same age. Vicious competition and unrelenting peer pressure are not unusual. Learning from peers can be like the blind leading the blind."

Of course, the proof of their argument is Sarah. She is an extremely social little girl. She appears to be very comfortable with people of all ages. Her ability to carry on a meaningful conversation with adults is truly extraordinary. She recently took part in a summer program for gifted children in which communication through creative writing was stressed. Sarah's teachers were most impressed with her intellectual abilities as well as her social interaction with other children.

WHAT OTHER PARENTS HAVE TO SAY

"We have some good teachers in our school, but they are overworked and underpaid. The pupil/teacher ratio is something like 28 to one. I don't care how good a teacher is, there is only so much time in so many days to give so much attention. At home, my children have a 3 to 1 ratio all the time." (New York)

"I really like home schooling because I really like teaching. Sometimes parents just like to work with their children, which may sound strange in this day and age." (Virginia)

"There really is no way that I would consider teaching my children at home. I don't feel qualified. I have a full-time job outside the home and wouldn't want to give up the personal satisfaction I receive from that experience. Besides, I just couldn't afford to stay home." (Illinois)

"Our city schools are full of problems of drugs, discipline, and declining achievement scores. The environment is just too cruel for my children. As long as we have the time and money, our children will be taught at home, at least until they reach high school." (Iowa)

"I think choosing to teach my children at home was the best possible decision for our family. We have strong Christian values and believe the public schools are just not equipped to meet our needs." (Ohio)

"Our children just didn't like school. Our son is gifted and the regimentation and control did not allow him to progress as fast as he was capable. However, the competition is what really turned us off. There are so many social clicks in our local school and we didn't want our children to learn in that situation." (Illinois)

SUGGESTIONS TO PARENTS

1. Do your homework! Research all you can about home schooling. Begin at the public library. Are there organizations and/or associations in your state concerned with home schooling? Such groups can serve as a clearinghouse for information. Many home schoolers get together from time to time to share their experiences. Do such organizations sponsor conferences, or conventions, training sessions?

2. Talk to parents who are presently engaged in home schooling. Experience is the best teacher! Most parents who advocate home schooling are pleased to share what they have learned.

3. Discuss your desire to educate your children at home with the local school officials. Take notes. Be prepared for positive and/or negative reactions. Your discussion should answer all your questions about the legalities involved. What tests/evaluation instruments are available and/or required?

4. Think it through. How much time will home schooling really take? What will it be like to spend 24 hours a day, nearly every day, with your children? What will be the cost of books and/or materials? What kind of support or criticism could you expect from local school officials, family members, or relatives?

5. Make a "contract" with your children stating your goals and objectives for home schooling.

6. Sharpen your own skills. Are there classes available at local colleges/universities that might help you improve your teaching skills or general knowledge? It is important to remember that if you want your child to enjoy being a lifelong learner, you must constantly MODEL that behavior.

7. What if your child has special needs, such as having a learning disability or hearing impairment? Will you be able to meet those needs at home? Could you work with the local schools in a cooperative effort to meet those needs?

8. Gather sample educational materials to review and evaluate. This process takes time! Many parents spend months on this task.

9. Be brave! Do what you feel is best for your children and yourself.

LET'S GET ORGANIZED!

Parent Advocacy in Gifted Education

An old and dear friend to gifted education, Mr. Yossel Naiman, once said, "Caring about appropriate education for gifted children is not enough unless that caring is translated into action." Of course Yossel was right. Real caring means saying something, writing something, doing something. Parent support groups for gifted education are truly the lifeline for gifted children in this country.

Wise educators know that gifted programs survive only with strong parent support. And, strong parent support that is **organized** translates into **power**—the power to motivate school boards, administrators, teachers, legislators, and businesspeople to each accept his/her own unique responsibility to gifted children.

HOW TO ORGANIZE A SUPPORT GROUP

1. Call together a meeting of a few concerned parents. You might also include educators, businesspeople, and PTA president. Try to keep this first meeting small.

2. Select a temporary chairperson and secretary.

3. Choose a topic and a speaker that will appeal to parents of the gifted for the next meeting. Set a date, place, and time.

4. Brainstorm a list of parents and teachers who might be interested in such a meeting and invite them. Send a notice of the meeting home with children from school. Be sure to ask your gifted coordinator, if you have one, for help. Set up a telephone committee to notify parents a few days before the meeting date. Publicize the meeting in the local newspaper.

5. Get a sign-up list of all those present. Be sure to get phone numbers!

6. Appoint a nominating committee to seek a slate of officers for the next meeting.

7. Survey those present regarding their special needs and interests as a guideline for programs and topics.

8. At the second meeting, discuss a name for your group, assess dues, and ask for volunteers for the following committees: program, membership, legislative, and constitution.

INFLUENCING PUBLIC POLICY AND LEGISLATION FOR GIFTED CHILDREN

Each year the plight of gifted programs is put into the hands of state lawmakers across this country. Parents of gifted children can influence legislation by applying pressure to the appropriate legislative committees in the form of letters, telephone calls, and visits to specific public officials. This influence takes time, energy, and persistence before results are seen in the form of new laws that mandate gifted education. (A certain amount of good old-fashioned tenacity doesn't hurt!) The name of the game is **communication.** Maintaining constant and open communication with legislators and public officials is probably the most effective way parents can motivate public policy concerning gifted children.

1. Write letters. Handwritten or typed letters are best. No form letters, please! Be specific, to the point, and brief. Share information about your gifted child and the needs of gifted education in your school district. If you are asking for support of a certain bill or policy, make sure you mention the number or code for that legislation. In general, be as well informed as possible about the issues concerning gifted education in your state. Offer to share more information upon request.

Send your letters to:

a. The Governor—Letters addressed to the governor should read:

The Honorable (Full name)
Office of the Governor
State Capitol Building
City, State, Zip

b. Senators and Representatives—The addresses for state and federal legislators may be obtained by calling your local newspaper or public library. Greetings to legislators should read "Dear Senator (full name)" or "Dear Representative (full name)".

c. Newspaper Editors—The "Letters to the Editor" column is an excellent way to share your feelings and ideas with many people. In addition, most public officials, legislators, and concerned citizens in general are faithful readers of the editorial page.

d. State Board of Education/State Superintendent of Schools

e. State Director or Coordinator of Gifted Education

2. Make Personal Visits to Legislators. This is probably the best way to show just how sincere and concerned you are as an advocate of gifted education. Nothing can take the place of a personal one-on-one dialogue concerning the issues. If possible, take your gifted child with you to the appointment.

3. Send a Mailgram. This is an excellent way to get your ideas across in a short, time-saving manner. It is a particularly useful method as a last minute reminder to legislators to vote on a particular piece of legislation.

4. Testify. Most parents fail to realize that there are usually several opportunities to share their views publicly at a House/Senate committee, commission, or special legislative hearing. Call or write the secretary of the House or the secretary of the Senate in your state capital for information concerning dates, times, and locations of such hearings.

5. Telephone. Calling government officials in order to state your opinion can be very helpful, especially if you have a specific piece of legislation coming up for a vote. Most public officials ask their staffs to keep a running tab of the pro and con comments concerning current bills. Be sure to mention the number of the bill when you call!

6. Draft a Bill. Yes, you can draft a bill! Sometimes the best way to influence legislation is to write it yourself. Once the bill is drafted, you must find a sponsor or sponsors among the senators and representatives from your district.

7. Invite public officials/legislators as speakers. The good news about this one is that it is free! Most public officials enjoy meeting and speaking to their public. Just make sure to ask for a date well in advance. Their calendars fill up in a hurry.

8. Vote. Use your power in the voting booth to effect changes for gifted children. Advocates of gifted education can be found in all areas of our society, even in government. Just remember, those found in the House and Senate are not made, they are elected!

SUGGESTIONS FOR WORKING WITH SCHOOL BOARDS

1. Attend a few board meetings and JUST LISTEN. Find out what it's like to be on a school board. Quite often, it is a thankless job for which few people volunteer. Most school board members are parents and taxpayers just like you, with concerns and worries about their children's education that are just as strong as yours. By attending a few meetings

before your actual presentation, you can learn who the officers are, how the meetings are conducted, and most importantly, which members seem to have the most power at influencing the others.

2. Do your HOMEWORK. You are not ready to make a presentation before the school board until you have gathered the facts and information to support your concerns. A supportive parent has influence. A supportive and informed parent has POWER—the power to motivate, the power to create or change policies.

First, find out exactly what is or isn't happening for gifted children in your district. There may be programs or activities happening for gifted children in classrooms other than your child's. Second, find out what is happening in other school districts in your state, especially those of similar size and financial status. Third, talk to other parents. A group presentation with one member serving as spokesperson might be effective. And it is a comfort to know you are not in this alone! Fourth, prepare a written HANDOUT, one for each board member that summarizes the facts and details about your concerns.

3. Get to KNOW the board members personally. Can you call the board members by their first names? Have you invited them over for coffee? Do you know their occupations? Have you given a board member a chance to know you personally?

4. Ask, in writing, ahead of time, to be placed on the agenda for the next board meeting. Most school boards stick to a prearranged agenda. Just because you show up at the meeting doesn't mean you will be given a chance to participate. Include in this written notice some of the issues you wish to raise with the board. This will allow the board members to prepare in advance some of their answers and spare them the embarrassment of being uninformed.

5. Offer suggestions. Nobody likes to listen to criticism from someone who offers no solutions. This is where your homework will come in handy. Offer several alternatives that the board may act on. Forcing one solution may only put them on the defensive.

IDEAS, ACTIVITIES, AND PROJECTS FOR PARENT SUPPORT GROUPS

- Sponsor workshops, conferences, and conventions.
- Compile a resource list of citizens willing to serve as mentors.
- Compile a resource list of people, places, and things for field trips.
- Sponsor a gifted fair to display and share talents of gifted children.
- Publish a newsletter.
- Attend school board meetings and present information on gifted education.
- Volunteer the services of parents as teacher aids.
- Present free memberships to legislators, public officials, and administrators.
- Provide information and/or sponsor summer programs for gifted children.
- Compile a resource list of books, periodicals, and journals related to gifted.
- Establish a PR committee to increase public awareness of gifted.
- Establish a legislative committee to explore funding possibilities.
- Publish a book of stories or poems written by gifted children.
- Invite experts in the field of gifted education to speak at meetings.
- Investigate and visit other gifted programs in other school districts.
- Become a clearinghouse for information and dates of conventions and workshops.
- Exchange ideas and information with other parent support groups.
- Provide articles for newspapers about gifted programs (include pictures).
- Publish a handbook for parents of gifted children.
- Support political candidates who advocate gifted education.
- Sponsor a young authors contest, creative problem solving bowl, and Olympics of the Mind.
- Raise money for scholarships for gifted children.
- Work with public libraries to provide special programs for gifted.
- Organize afterschool and/or Saturday minicourses for gifted.

RESOURCES

American Young Mensa
c/o MENSA
50 East 42nd Street
New York, NY 10017

Creative Education Foundation
State University College at Buffalo
1300 Elmwood Avenue
Buffalo, NY 14222

National Association for Creative Children and
Adults
8080 Spring Valley Drive
Cincinnati, OH 45236

National Association for Gifted Children
1155 15th Street NW
Suite #1002
Washington D.C. 20005

National/State Leadership Training Institute (LTI)
316 West Second Street PH-C
Los Angeles, CA 90012

S.E.N.G. (Supporting Emotional Needs of Gifted)
Ellis Human Development Institute
9 North Edwin C. Moses Blvd.
Dayton, OH 45407

The Association for the Gifted (TAG)
Council for Exceptional Children
1920 Association Drive
Reston, VA 22091

The Illinois Association for Gifted Children
POB 2451
Grenview IL 60025

Gifted Association of Missouri
P.O. Box 1495
Jefferson City, MO 65102

Parenting Skills for the 90s: Your Gifted Child
(VHS) $29.95 by Nancy L. Johnson
Pieces of Learning
1610 Brook Lynn Drive
Beavercreek OH 45432   1-800-729-5137

The Survival Guide for Parents of Gifted Kids
by Sally Walker
Free Spirit Publishing
400 1st Avenue North Suite 616
Minneapolis MN 55401

CHALLENGE (magazine)
Good Apple, Inc.
P.O. Box 299
Carthage, IL 62321

Roper Review (journal)
Roeper City and County School
2190 North Woodward
Bloomfield Hills, MI 48013

The Gifted Child Today (magazine)
Prufrock Press
POB 8813
Waco TX 76714

Understanding Our Gifted (newsletter)
P.O. Box 3489
Littleton, CO 80161

How to Be a Gifted Parent
by David Lewis
(Norton Press, 1979)

*Somewhere to Turn: Strategies for Parents of
Gifted and Talented Children*
(Teachers College Press, 1980)

Getting Schools Involved with Parents
R.L. Kroth
(Council for Exceptional Children, 1978.)

A SURVIVAL KIT FOR PARENTS OF GIFTED CHILDREN

A few years ago, a popular disco song recorded by Gloria Gaynor professed the confident title "I Will Survive!" At the time, it seemed like a perfect theme song for parents of gifted children. The joys and frustrations of living with a gifted child must surely cause parents to wonder, "WILL I survive?" In fact, raising a gifted child might well be the greatest test of parenting skills that exists! It is easy to identify parents of gifted children because they quite often give themselves away. When a parent approaches with a worried look, a smile, and a tired shaky voice, it usually means, "Help, I think I'm the parent of a gifted child!"

The tired voice reminds me of the energy, both physical and emotional, that it must take to parent gifted children. "This kid just wears me out!" is a frequent comment. The worried look in the eyes reminds me of the intense concern parents have for the future of their gifted children and the desperation and frustration they feel with the school and community. The smiles on their faces remind me of the pride parents must feel in their gifted children, a pride that is easily held inside but sometimes hard to express in public.

If a survival kit for parents of gifted children existed to help the worried eyes, tired voices, and smiling faces, the contents might include the following:

PLAYING CARD

Card games can serve many useful purposes for you and your gifted child.

1. Playing card games will stretch a child's attention span, concentration skills, short-term memory, and math ability. (*Deal Me In!* by Margie Golick, Jeffrey Norton Publishing, 145 East 49th St., New York, NY 10017.)

2. Conversation is sometimes easier over a game of cards. Besides stretching logical thinking skills, the cards can serve as a communication tool. Words and feelings seem to flow more freely when two people are playing cards. Family activities are important learning experiences for gifted children. However, it is just as important for your gifted child to be involved in one-on-one activities with each parent. So, how about turning off the TV for a little while? How about a game of cards?

3. Remember, conversation means listening as well as talking. LISTEN! There are times when your gifted child needs your undivided attention to his/her perceptions, questions, and concerns.

BIRTHDAY CANDLE

The birthday candle symbolizes surprises. Unfortunately, gifted children can suffer from depression just like other children. In fact, many gifted children are worriers. The problem is that they worry about the "big stuff:" world peace, starvation in Africa, the energy crisis, etc. At times, it all gets to be too much, and they get really "down in the dumps." One way to shake children loose from some of those feelings is to try and get them to talk about it. Verbalizing all those worries can really help. Another way to boost your child's spirits is to surprise him/her. A father of one of the gifted children in my class surprised his son one day by showing up in the school cafeteria for lunch. The boy was so proud and pleased that his father would take time from work to surprise him by coming to school. The euphoria from that quick lunch lasted for days. It was like having a new student in my class! On another occasion, a parent mailed her child's birthday present to school. What a surprise when the mail carrier delivered the gift! Surprises can take many forms: trips, gifts, telephone calls, rearranged furniture, etc. They work like magic!

PAPER SACK

This is a very special paper sack. It's used to throw away bad behavior. Adults quite often expect gifted children to behave better than other children. We should not expect adult behavior from a child even though at times the child may talk or think like an adult. Sometimes we remind the child of past misbehavior and "hold it over his/her head." At the same time, we remind the child that he/she is gifted. Example: "Mary, that's the fourth time you've done that. Now stop it! I've told you four times to stop that. You re supposed to be gifted! You should know better!" After a time, Mary might begin to relate bad behavior with being gifted. As a parent, learn to discipline your child, deal with the problem, then throw it away. Being reminded of past mistakes can be just as embarrassing and painful to children as to adults.

RUBBER BAND

Your gifted child is like a rubber band. Rubber bands can be stretched in different directions. It doesn't hurt them-that's what they are for! As a parent, try to stretch your gifted child in different directions.

1. Encourage the child to spend time with other gifted people. Remember, your child has two sets of peers: age peers and intellectual peers. There should be time for interaction with both.

2. Go! Go! Go to the museum, public library, concerts, sporting events, grandma's house, circus, zoo, campground, lectures, movies, etc. Your gifted child needs a variety of experiences.

3. Encourage your child to participate in activities that might stretch talent development: music lessons, tumbling class, community theater, clubs and organizations.

4. Provide stretching materials and equipment in the home: art supplies, building materials, musical instruments, electronic equipment, resource books, complex games (Chess, Mastermind, Othello), chemistry set, special interest magazines, etc. Be sure to include materials that develop imagination and imagery, such as fairy tales, open-ended stories, folktales, myths, fables, or nature books.

5. Support your gifted child when he/she succeeds as well as when he/she fails. Stretching is a risky business! Create an atmosphere where risk taking is OK!

6. Permit time for thinking and daydreaming. Just because children might not look like they are busy doesn't mean that their minds are not.

REFRIGERATOR SIGN

Place an index card on the refrigerator with the following words printed on it: LOVING, LAUGHING, and LEARNING.

LOVING: Sometimes we need to be reminded of the obvious. Your gifted child is a child first and gifted second. Have you talked with your child about the term "gifted" and what it means? Have you told your child it's OK to be gifted? Have you explained that being gifted doesn't mean you are better than other people, just different? Have you said **I LOVE YOU?**

LAUGHING: Whatever happens, don't lose your sense of humor! Don't take your gifted child too seriously. There are times when your gifted child will do things that might seem a bit out of character. Just because your child has a gifted mind doesn't mean he/she has gifted behavior, a gifted mouth, a gifted body, or gifted handwriting!

LEARNING: Some parents believe that home is where you live and school is where you learn. Your home is also a learning environment. As models, parents and other family members are constantly teaching the gifted child. Educating gifted children is a TEAM EFFORT involving teachers and parents in the learning process. Look out! Someone's watching! Someone's LEARNING!

KITE STRING

Gifted children are like kites-they are meant to be lifted! Sometimes it's hard to let go of a kite, allowing it to go higher and higher, watching it float farther and farther away. But that's what kites are supposed to do. Sometimes it's hard to watch your gifted child being "lifted," stretching and taking risks with his/her life. It's important that gifted children possess a certain amount of intellectual, emotional, and physical mobility. Some gifted adults are notorious for changing professions several times in their lifetimes. Just as a kite moves in several directions, the gifted child must also be prepared to change positions and interests. It all adds up to something we educators call "flexibility."

QUESTION: What happens when a kite goes too high or drifts near a dangerous power line?

ANSWER: We pull back on the string. As a parent, don't be afraid to pull back once in a while. Don't be intimidated by your gifted child. He/She needs discipline and guidance just like other children.

GIFTED KIDS AND KITES ARE MEANT TO BE LIFTED BUT DON'T LET GO OF THE STRING!

TELEVISION SIGN

How much TV does your child watch? Most children watch in excess of forty hours a week. Does the TV act as a human baby-sitter? Is the TV the most important piece of furniture in your living room? How many TV's does your family own?

A few years ago, the National Parent/Teacher Association recommended that each television have a card sitting on top with the following words printed on it: WHO, WHAT, WHEN, WHERE, and WHY. They suggested that, as children were watching, adults should ask questions using one or more of these words. It forces the child to verbalize what he/she is watching and breaks the hypnotic effect that TV has on the child's learning process. Some of the child's answers may surprise you! (*The Plug-In Drug* by Marie Winn, Viking Press, 625 Madison Ave., New York, NY 10022.)

LOLLIPOP

Many parents wage a continuing battle against refined sugar. If it is true that we are what we eat, then parents should constantly be aware of their child's eating habits. The lollipop is 99 percent refined sugar and 1

percent color additive. The problem is in the total amount of sugar your child gets in one day. There are various kinds of sugar in so many of the convenience foods that we eat, the amount begins to build in a hurry! If your gifted child has a hyperactive mind and body, he/she might be affected by the amount of sugar he/she consumes in a day. Educators are warned against teaching new skills the week after Halloween or the week after Easter. Some children do not retain what they have been taught during those weeks. A "big charge" of sugar seems to short circuit the memory process, and those new skills have to be retaught.

No parent wants his/her child, gifted or otherwise, to become "Junk Food Junkies." Most gifted children read at an early age. So teach them to read labels. Teach them early what good nutrition is all about. The best way to do this is by setting a good example! (*Sugar Blues* by William Dufty, Warner Press, 1976, New York, N.Y. *The Taming of the C.A.N.D.Y. Monster* by Vicki Lansky, Meadowbrook Press, 1978, Wayzata, MN)

BROKEN PENCIL

The pencil is a symbol for academic learning activities, the kind most children experience in school. Yes, the pencil is broken. Quite often, parents expect more paper/pencil homework when they discover their child is gifted. "Shouldn't this child be doing more work sheets if he/she is gifted?" is a frequent comment from parents and teachers. **GIFTED CHILDREN DO NOT NEED MORE OF THE SAME OLD THING-THEY NEED DIFFERENT!**

There are so many other things parents can do at home other than paper/pencil activities. That is why the pencil is broken. Put clay in your child's hands or a violin or checkers or a puppy or your own hands! Think about all the learning experiences that can't take place in the regular classroom. Those are the experiences parents should try to provide at home.

DO NOT DISTURB

There are times when gifted children are truly delightful, amazing human beings who constantly surprise us with their abilities. Isn't it wonderful! However, there are also times when gifted children are the nosiest, most demanding little critters who ever invaded our lives! They seem to delight in driving the adult world crazy! Some gifted children are nonstop talkers, asking what seems like a thousand questions a day. The use of a DO NOT DISTURB sign can really be a godsend. Teaching your gifted child the meaning of the sign and why it is important to respect it may be an important survival skill for all parents. (**NOTE:** Be sure to stress to your child that the DO NOT DISTURB sign does not mean that you don't love him/her; it just means that you don't want to be close to him/her for a little while.) There need be only three reasons for not respecting the sign: Fire, Blood, or Throwing Up! Most parents agree that just about anything else can wait!

P.S. Children should have their own DO NOT DISTURB signs too.

RESOURCES

Coffey, Kay, Gina Ginsberg, Carrol Lockhart, Carol Nathan, Delois McCartney, and Keith Wood. *Parents Speak on Gifted and Talented Children.* Order from LTI Publications, Ventura County Superintendent of Schools, County Office Building, Ventura, CA 93001.

Delp, Jeanne L., and Ruth A. Martinson. *A Handbook for Parents of Gifted and Talented* Order from LTI Publications.

Dickinson, Rita. *Caring for the Gifted.* North Quincy, MA: Christopher Publishing, 1970.

Eberle, R. *Scamper: Games for Imagination Development,* Buffalo, NY: D.O.K. Publishers, Inc., 1971.

Gallagher, J.J. *Teaching the Gifted Child,* Second Edition. Boston: Allyn, Bacon & Company, 1975.

Ginsberg, Gina, and Charles H. Harrison. *How to Help Your Gifted Child: A Handbook for Parents and Teachers.* The Gifted Child Society, Inc. Order from Monarch Press, 1 West 39th St., New York, NY 10018.

Kanigher, Herbert. *Everyday Enrichment for Gifted Children at Home and School.* Order from LTI Publications.

Kaufmann, Felice. *Your Gifted Child and You.* Order from the Council for Exceptional Children, 1920 Association Drive, Reston, VA 22091.

Pickard, Phyllis M. *If You Think Your Child Is Gifted.* Order from Linnet Books, The Shoe String Press, P.O. Box 4327, 955 Sherman Avenue, Hamden, CT 06514.

A Special Note to Teachers and Administrators: The Survival Kit works well as a handout for parent workshops. The contents are inexpensive and the kits can easily be assembled in one evening. Each item in the kit serves as a visual symbol related to the ideas you are trying to share during the workshop. Parents enjoy taking the Survival Kit home to serve as a reminder during future times when things get rough!

TAKING TIME TO COMMUNICATE

Calendar Notes for Busy Parents

My Grandma Ona managed to repeat the following bit of advice several times to her oldest granddaughter: "If you want something done—give it to a busy person." That probably explains how so many parents of gifted children have managed to accomplish so much in the past few years as advocates of gifted education. Today's family members seem more involved in individual interests and activities than ever before. Consequently, the skills of planning, organizing, and managing such busy families become even more important. The fact that some members of the family are gifted only increases the problem!

To the parents of gifted children, the word "communication" is synonymous with "advocacy." To be an advocate of gifted education takes TIME. Specifically, it takes TIME TO COMMUNICATE.

First, and most important, there must be open and continuous communication between parent and child. Second, there must be spoken and written channels of communication developed between parents and educators. And third, there must be free and open communication with other parents of gifted children.

The following suggestions are presented to help busy parents MAKE time for communication. These calendar notes can be cut apart and attached to a regular calendar on appropriate days throughout the year. It is hoped they will serve as continuous reminders to busy parents as they fulfill their responsibilities as "gifted parents."

104

SUN	MON	TUE	WED	THU	FRI	SAT
	Help plan and organize a **Future Problem-Solving Program**					
				Join a **national organization** concerned with gifted children.		

Call _____'s teacher and ask to **ATTEND SCHOOL**. Make an appointment for parent/teacher conferences.

Write to the nearest **College or University** and ask to be placed on their mailing list for notification of future concerts, lectures, seminars, stage plays and sporting events.

Begin keeping a journal. Include comments on _____'s interests, projects feelings about school attitudes about self Share journal at parent/teacher conference

Attend a School Board **Meeting**
Time:
Place:
Call _____ and invite them to attend.

Read *What Makes You So Special* by Sherri Heller: Thinking CAPS PO Box 7230 Phoenix AZ 85001

Thought for the day: **LIVING WITH GIFTED CHILDREN TAKES TIME** *ENERGY* *PATIENCE* and a **SENSE OF HUMOR**

WRITE to the "Letters to the Editor" column in the local newspaper in support of gifted programs **Address:**

105

SUN	MON	TUE	WED	THU	FRI	SAT
		RAID the local **toy store** for future birthday and Christmas presents.				

Write to the president of the nearest college or university and encourage him to offer **CLASSES** for parents and teachers in gifted education. Help advertise the availability of these courses.

Volunteer to edit a **NEWSLETTER** on gifted education for parents & educators.

Monitor the amount of **TELEVISION** that the whole family watches this week. Discuss the results at a **family conference.**

Declare this week: **BETTER LISTENING WEEK** Repeat the following promise several times this week: I promise to be a better listener when _____ talks to me.

Write to the State Superintendent of Schools and ask for a list of gifted programs in the state. **GO VISIT ONE** Address: Call the principal first.

THOUGHT FOR THE WEEK "Locked up in the mind of my gifted child is.. ...an answer ...a cure ...a MIRACLE

Begin today to **BE A BETTER MODEL** for my gifted child. Sign up for an adult education class at the nearest community college. Or run for a public office. The school board is a good place to start.

THE COFFEE-TABLE CHRISTMAS

The most important lessons of life are those taught by the most important teachers — parents. They are usually gentle lessons, taught in the simplest context at the most unexpected times — yet resulting in a profound and lasting impression.

It began December 1, when the fullness of Thanksgiving had worn off and the air began to really feel like winter. It was a tight, tingling feeling in the top part of my stomach that pushed against my lungs, forcing an extra breath now and then. I was six years old, and CHRISTMAS WAS COMING! It was everywhere, an incredible excitement. You could feel it, see it, touch it, and smell it. There surely must be something special, a magic combination, between childhood and Christmas. Of course, adults were affected too. Mrs. Stevenson, my teacher, was smiling all the time, motivated no doubt by a sudden rash of good behavior exhibited by her students following a class letter to Santa Claus. (Surely Santa would remember all our good deeds and overlook a few minor indiscretions!) The requests for presents covered several pages; my list was among the longest. It seemed like the whole world was turning around me, getting ready to celebrate with me, purchasing gifts for me. Yes, I was reminded in Sunday School that our gifts to one another were really symbols of gifts to the Christ Child. But when you are six years old and you know there will be dolls and games and toys and maybe even a pony on Christmas morning—well, it's hard to focus on "the giving" when your mind is bursting with "the getting." By the third week in December, it was all I could do to just go to bed, let alone sleep when I got there.

It was an especially cold winter. Our farm had been covered with a thick, glazed blanket of snow for weeks. I remember how the snow cracked and squeaked under my feet in the sub-zero mornings as I walked from the house to the corncrib to do my chores. The corncrib was my favorite place on the farm. It was a place to work and play, a place to dream, and a place to share thoughts and feelings with special friends.

When you are a farm kid, with no brothers or sisters, and you live several miles from town, your special friends are critters—so you talk to them. Brownie knew just what I wanted for Christmas. He'd bark and wag his tail when I would describe in great detail, including hand signals and sound effects, all the toys I had asked for. And I knew that Snowball's silky white fur felt just like the hair of that Tony doll I had picked out of the catalog. She'd purr and stretch when I talked about the tea parties the three of us would have. The pattern was set: there would be time to decorate the house, time for church on Christmas Eve, time for a big dinner, and time for me to open my presents!

Then, unexpectedly, the pattern changed. It was three days before Christmas. I looked out my bedroom window because Brownie was barking. Dad had just come home from town and had parked the pickup truck down by the corncrib instead of up by the house. My mom didn't notice because she was in the basement washing clothes. Dad hollered for me from the porch. "Get your duds on and come out to the crib," he said. "Hurry up!" I didn't know what was going on. But when your dad is 6'6" tall and weighs over 200 pounds and says hurry up—you hurry up! I pulled on my snowsuit in record time, tugged at my boots, and ran out the door, fumbling with my mittens and scarf. Brownie had beaten me to the crib by 30 seconds and was sitting patiently at Dad's feet waiting for me. Dad proceeded to unload a large, strange-looking object from the pickup. Before I had time to ask, he said, "It's a new coffee table for your mom. We can

surprise her with it on Christmas morning." My eyes grew wide with excitement as he tore a bit of the protective paper from one corner so I could see it. The wood was a beautiful mahogany, so shiny and smooth that it reflected the light like a mirror. "What do ya think?" he asked. "Isn't it somethin'? Pretty fancy, huh?" I'm not sure which is more vivid in my memory, the glow of that wood or of Dad's smile! In either case, it was a very special moment. The next few seconds were filled with hugs, squeals of joy, lots of jumping up and down, and a barking dog! When things settled down, we carefully placed the plainly wrapped treasure on a pile of corn in the corner of the crib. "Now don't let on to your mom what's out here!" Dad said. "It's a surprise, remember?" My eyes met Dad's and we both smiled again. It was the first real secret we had ever shared.

Brownie tilted his head first one way then the other, looking at the strange object that had invaded his territory. He sniffed the paper and licked the string trying to understand why two humans made such a fuss over something that wasn't even fit to eat! I shook my finger at his nose, lectured him about the

108

expense of fine furniture, and threatened him with all sorts of punishments if he even got near it.

The next three days were filled with new emotions as well as several trips to the corncrib—just to check on things! I was also experiencing some new and different feelings of anticipation. My excitement about Christmas was stronger than ever, but the tingling sensation pushing against my lungs no longer reminded me of all the presents waiting for me. All I thought about was Mom and that coffee table. The day before Christmas, I took Snowball with me to the crib. I told her all about the surprise—how the wood felt just as smooth and silky as her fur and how I could hardly wait to see the look on Mom's face when she saw the coffee table for the first time.

When Christmas morning finally arrived, I bounded down the stairs to find Mom and Dad eating breakfast at the kitchen table. I headed straight for the porch and my snowsuit and boots. Mom seemed surprised that I was more interested in getting dressed to go outside than I was in opening gifts. "Don't you want to look under the Christmas tree?" she asked. "I think there are some presents there for you." As I tugged at my boots, I replied, "Later! Dad and I have to go outside and get something. Come on, Dad. Hurry up! HURRY up!" (When your six-year-old daughter wants to race out into sub-zero weather, skip breakfast, delay opening her Christmas gifts, and insists that you hurry up—you hurry up!)

I ran to the crib, beating Brownie by 30 seconds, all the time hollering to Dad to hurry even more. Finally, Dad carried the brown, strangely shaped object to the house and waited with it on the porch while I made Mom sit in the living room with her eyes closed. Then into the living room came the brown object, the father, the kid, the dog, the cat, and lots of dripping snow! SURPRISE! Mom gently unwrapped the table, treating the brown paper as carefully as she would the most expensive tissue. As the shining mahogany began to reveal itself, my mother's face became more beautiful than I had ever remembered it. A glow of surprise mixed with tears and smiles covered her face. There were many feelings spoken but no words. Between the "ooh's" and "ahh's" she first gently stroked the coffee table, then my head, and then my father's face.

For the first time in my young life, I had experienced the pride and pure joy that gift giving can bring. My father had taught me an important lesson that cold December, a lesson about giving and receiving, a lesson that repeated itself every time I saw my mother dust that coffee table. There were other gifts that Christmas morning, but what they were and who received them was lost in the warm glow of mahogany.

MERRY CHRISTMAS, DAD!

Thinking is the Key — is a practical resource for teaching critical thinking in different ways. It includes hundreds of divergent questions and activities to supplement basic curriculum. Ideas and activities motivate both reluctant learners and high achievers with chapters focusing on global education, the environment, color, and visual and kinesthetic thinking. Nancy includes an evaluation tool that teachers and administrators can use to assess teacher questioning effectiveness. K-12 Educators, college teachers, parents, and home educators will find this a valuable resource for fostering life long thinking. Reproducibles. **96p.**   ISBN 1-880505-01-0 $9.95   **K-12**   CLC0144

Questioning Makes the Difference explores the types of questions educators can use to stimulate **high-level thinking**. These kinds of questions encourage students to analyze problems, pull together knowledge from various content areas, and evaluate answers. Nancy gives hundreds of examples of questions educators can use in daily lessons. Includes reproducibles. The book complements both videos *Teaching Skills for the 90s.*   80 p.   ISBN 0-9623835-3-8 $8.95   **K-12**   CLC0072

Teaching Skills for the 90s: Strategies and Activities to Stimulate High-level Thinking *(VHS)* is a 3 segment, three-hour workshop in which Nancy interacts with an audience to illustrate ways of stimulating high-level thinking. Nancy specifically addresses **creating** the possibility for students to think in different ways, **learning** to ask different kinds of questions, and **applying** knowledge in different ways. The video complements the books *Questioning Makes the Difference* and *Thinking is the Key.*
ISBN 0-9623835-4-6   **Staff Development** $79.95   **K-12**   CLC0082

Teaching Skills for the 90s: Questioning Makes the Difference *(VHS)* is a 100-minute segment of the Strategies and Activities video described above. This interactive tape contains discussion and illustration of questioning. Nancy shares four kinds of questions that stimulate high-level thinking in students. The video complements the books *Questioning Makes the Difference* and *Thinking is the Key.*
ISBN 0-9623835-5-4   **Staff Development** $49.95   **K-12**   CLC0073

Parenting Skills for the 90s: The Parenting Puzzle—Piece by Piece *(VHS)*   is a 90 minute, 2 segment interactive seminar. The first segment focuses on the parent as role model and teacher and offers techniques that build positive self esteem in children. The second segment asks parents to explore the skills children need to become life long learners. Nancy shares ideas about traditions, consistency, secrets, problems, heroes, responsibility, overparenting, safe rebellion, health and other 90s' attitudes and concerns.
In-home and Educator/Parent In-service.
ISBN 1-88505-00-2 $39.95   CLC0116

Parenting Skills for the 90s: Your Gifted Child *(VHS)* is a 3 segment 90-minute video in which Nancy addresses concerns educators and parents have about gifted learners. The video's initial segment lists and discusses observable characteristics of gifted children. Nancy guides viewers into a better understanding of gifted children and adult responsibilities to them. The second segment presents techniques for surviving the joys and frustrations of having a gifted child. In the third segment, Nancy discusses the more difficult issues we must deal with in the 90s and the communication skills critical to positive interaction with this decade's gifted learners. Complements the book *The Faces of Gifted.*
In-home and Educator/Parent In-Service Education
ISBN 0-9623835-1-1 $29.95   CLC0098